EAST & WEST

COMPARATIVE STUDIES IN PURSUIT OF TRADITION

by

JULIUS EVOLA

EDITED BY GREG JOHNSON & COLLIN CLEARY

Counter-Currents Publishing Ltd.
San Francisco
2018

Cover image:
Rembrandt, *Philosopher in Meditation*, 1632
Musée du Louvre

Cover design by
Kevin I. Slaughter

Published in the United States by
COUNTER-CURRENTS PUBLISHING LTD.
P.O. Box 22638
San Francisco, CA 94122
USA
http://www.counter-currents.com/

Hardcover ISBN: 978-1-935965-66-4
Paperback ISBN: 978-1-935965-67-1
E-book ISBN: 978-1-935965-68-8

Library of Congress Cataloging-in-Publication Data

Names: Evola, Julius, 1898-1974. | Johnson, Greg, 1971- editor. | Cleary,
  Collin, 1973- editor.
Title: East and west : comparative studies in pursuit of tradition / Julius
  Evola ; edited by Greg Johnson and Collin Cleary.
Description: San Francisco : Counter-Currents Publishing, 2013. | Includes
  bibliographical references and index.
Identifiers: LCCN 2013014905 (print) | LCCN 2013022700 (ebook) | ISBN
  9781935965688 (epub) | ISBN 9781935965664 (hardcover : alk. paper) | ISBN
  9781935965671 (pbk. : alk. paper)
Subjects: LCSH: Tradition (Philosophy) | Tradition (Theology) | Philosophy. |
  Religions.
Classification: LCC B105.T7 (ebook) | LCC B105.T7 E96 2015 (print) | DDC
  109--dc23
LC record available at https://lccn.loc.gov/2013014905

CONTENTS

FOREWORD

East and West collects eighteen essays and reviews by Julius Evola published in the journal *East and West* from 1950 to 1960. *East and West* was edited by Giuseppe Tucci and published by the Italian-based Institute for the Study of the Middle and Far East (Istituto di Studi per il Medio e l'Estremo Oriente, ISMEO). *East and West* published works by leading scholars of Eastern and Western thought, including Mircea Eliade, Franz Altheim, and Lionello Lanciotti.

East and West was published in English. Evola wrote his articles in Italian, and they were translated anonymously by one or more translators. Evola's Italian originals are no longer extant, which is a pity, because the quality of the translations is uneven, and some passages are obviously just wrong. However, even in the absence of the originals, it was still possible for us to render the texts in more lucid and idiomatic English.

Other difficult passages were clarified by consulting the Italian reverse translation of these pieces published as *Oriente e Occidente* (*Saggi vari*), ed. and trans. Gianluca Niccoletti and Marco Pucciarini (La Queste, 1984). Although the Italian translation is not an authoritative original, it is still a highly intelligent interpretation of the English texts by scholars who have a solid understanding of Evola's thought and who are fluent in his mother tongue. In the end, however, a few baffling sentences remain.

These pieces are ordered chronologically, with one exception. We switched the order of the first two chapters, because the second essay published makes an ideal first chapter, as it introduces Evola's overall analytical framework and many of the themes treated in subsequent chapters. The chapter titles are Evola's, with the exception of chapters 8, 11, and 16. Chapters 8 and 11 are book reviews and were published without titles. We gave chapter 16 a descriptive subtitle.

The main title of this book is, of course, the title of the original journal. The subtitle, "Comparative Studies in Pursuit of

Tradition" is our own description of Evola's basic method and orientation. Evola's comparative studies in Eastern and Western philosophy, religion, and mysticism were not motivated by a desire to facilitate political and cultural "dialogue" between the modern East and the modern West. Nor was he interested in superficial correspondences between academic philosophies and exoteric religions. He regarded these correspondences as manifestations of a deeper unity. Unlike C. G. Jung, however, Evola did not think that this unity arose from "subpersonal" or "chthonic" forces but were, instead, remnants of a common, primordial spiritual Tradition which influenced both Eastern and Western philosophical schools and religions.

Evola followed René Guénon in his belief that this primordial Tradition has been severed in the West, leaving only dead and decontextualized fragments. But they believed that the Tradition remained alive in the East. Thus those who wish to recover the Traditions of the West must look to the East to recover the esoteric teachings that provide the animating principle necessary to breathe new life and meaning into the dried remnants of the Tradition in the West. Although, as Evola argues presciently in his essay on Guénon, the rapid "Westernization" of the East may lead to a reversal, in which Easterners will have to go West to find the sparks with which to rekindle their own traditions.

I wish to thank my co-editor Collin Cleary as well as John Morgan, Bryan Sylvain, Matthew Peters, James J. O'Meara, A. Graham, Kevin Slaughter, Tim R., and Michael Polignano for their assistance with this edition.

Greg Johnson
February 17, 2018

THE LIBERATING INFLUENCES OF THE TRADITIONAL EAST

The relationship between East and West, particularly with regard to the influence each exercises over the other, has of late frequently been taken into consideration, but, in my opinion, the conclusions drawn have hardly ever been satisfactory. This is due to the absence of a comprehensive appreciation of the real terms of the problem. The first thing to decide is what is meant by the general terms "East" and "West," taking into account historical as well as other factors, since civilizations are never static. They develop and may undergo changes so radical that the East of our day is not, for instance, the East of the past, while the West of today differs from the West of even recent times. This is sufficient to explain the fact that the use of stereotyped designations is likely to lead to confusing things that are actually quite different from each other.

This is a point of great importance to those who affect to perceive a fundamental difference, if not a dialectical incompatibility, between East and West. This is what happens whenever an unwarranted identification is made of Western civilization with what can be defined only as modern civilization, which is obviously more and more difficult to identify with one continent or group of peoples, inasmuch as it is rapidly spreading over the whole world, displaying much the same characteristics everywhere. In the East, too, modern civilization has been gaining ground, not only in the realms of politics and social organization. It has also acquired a hold on the Oriental mind; many Orientals have succumbed to the mirage of "Europeanization" and boast of having acquired a "Western" mentality, culture, and way of life.

These recent aspects of an East already altered through contact with the West do not come, of course, within our purview, for if we were to consider them, all contrasts between the two civilizations would be effaced. Indeed, we are daily witnessing not only how Orientals, suitably conditioned and trained along these lines, are quite capable of displaying the same dynamic and military qualities which were until recently considered to be the exclusive property of the Western peoples, as well as the very opposite of the alleged inertia, the passive and contemplative orientation of the Asiatic races. We are also witnessing not a few Orientals falling into step with the Westerners, even in matters of technology, scientific research, and economics. This marks a stage in a general process towards standardization, the ultimate effect of which is bound eventually to divest the terms "East" and "West" of their present respective significance; they will survive only as geographical expressions.[1]

But there exists, of course, an authentic East apart from all this. It is the "Traditional East," and it should be carefully distinguished from the more or less modernized forms of Asiatic civilization. What relation can be traced between this Traditional East and our own civilization? If by the expression "our civilization" we mean "*modern* civilization," undoubtedly we find a marked difference between the two. Many, however, who start from this premise, end by rejecting the claims of the so-called "defenders of the West." Noting the materialistic, individualistic, and rationalistic trends of the modern Western world, these critics are inclined to think of the East as the center of a possible spiritual influence, which they however conceive almost always in confused and muddled terms, very often selecting as references doubtful, distorted, or ill-understood aspects of the spiritual life of the East. An instance of this is afforded by Anglo-Indian Theosophy and by various currents of humanitarian or pantheistic Spiritualism which have grown up on the margin of our civilization. As a matter of fact, it may be asked whether persons entertaining such ideas would not do better to get a clearer understanding of a heritage they have forgotten, before they speak of the East of which they know so little and only at second or third hand, and which they ap-

---

[1] Japan until lately afforded an interesting example of an Eastern people which held on to its spiritual tradition in spite of being widely Westernized in its outer life. Japan having been overthrown, it is difficult to tell how far it would have been able to maintain that position.

proach in a spirit of escapism. Only then could their contact with the spiritual forces of the East act not as a purely external influence, but as a fulfilment based on real understanding and intellectual sympathy.

It is a fact that a philosophy and a morphology of culture, capable of overcoming the historical and illuministic prejudices of the current academic mentality, would soon discover that the real difference lies not between Oriental and Western civilization, but rather between the modern pattern of civilization as a whole and what we may call the Traditional one, which in its essentials and under various forms, is the same in East and West. While the West throughout its history has gradually detached itself from the Traditional type of civilization, and to such an extent that even the recollection of it has been lost or radically modified, the East has remained faithful to Tradition and until lately, at least, has given evidence of this fidelity in forms still unpolluted, drawing their inspiration from its original sources. Paul Dahlke was, therefore, right when he said, with reference to certain metaphysical teachings, that the East still remembers what the West once possessed but has forgotten.[2] The distance between East and West is fundamentally that which separates two different phases of one and the same civilization: namely, the modern phase and the Traditional one in general, which lasted in Europe until medieval universality came to an end.

A split has since occurred in the West which has been broadening with amazing rapidity. That split has given rise to a new, unprecedented world which has chosen for itself a questionable direction leading to a new civilization from which all transcendental metaphysical elements, all elements not purely

---

[2] Evola, in his *The Doctrine of Awakening: The Attainment of Self-Mastery According to the Earliest Buddhist Texts*, trans. H. E. Musson (Rochester, Vt.: Inner Traditions, 1996), cites on p. 9 (note 14) Paul Dahlke, *Buddhismus als Religion und Moral* (Munich-Neubiberg: Oskar Schloss, 1923). — Eds.

human, have been gradually eliminated. As long as we cling to this world and consider ourselves the children of this civilization, adapting ourselves fully to the modern mentality and all it implies, with no understanding of any higher spiritual dignity, all endeavors to come closer to the East will be in vain, for whatever we touch will be distorted and defiled. No creative results will be achieved, since the condition for such achievement is a process from the interior, the influence of like on like, the reaction of like before like.

The matter stands on a rather different footing if we take into consideration the terminal phase of modern Western civilization, with its evident forms of crisis and dissolution on the one hand, while on the other new forces are set free and come to the fore. We would call these forces elemental rather than intellectual; although in the West they have found frequent expression in the domain of thought and culture, the cases with which we are concerned are not those of mere intellectual criticism and more or less brilliant personal considerations on the present crisis, such as are to be found in many of the books now in vogue. The problem to be faced is *how* to guide these forces and how to integrate their possibilities.

We believe that the frame of reference for this should be provided by ideas and notions having the character of "Traditional constants," that is to say, such spiritual elements as, in the East and in the West of a former day, have varied only in their external and historical forms of expression and application. The fundamental aim to be attained in this way consists in precipitating what we could call a "break in level." We will try briefly to illustrate our meaning, though we are now entering on what is virtually unexplored territory to the great majority of our Western contemporaries.

The difficulty lies in the fact that modern man has shut himself in a sort of magic circle and is incapable of conceiving and appreciating any values other than purely human ones. It follows that almost all the categories generally used in the West to describe those aspects of the East that are pure, authentic, and Traditional, are inadequate for their object and give rise to misunderstanding. It is necessary, first of all, to realize that the spirituality we are dealing with has nothing in common with philosophy. The East has, of course, produced forms of philosophy such as the Upanishads, the works of Nagarjuna, or Al-Ghazali, etc. But, apart from occasional exceptions, such works are philosophies in form only, and their essence is derived from a super-rational and super-individual plane. They are not the result of subjective speculation, but of objective experience warranted by a millennial tradition. The dependence of philosophical forms on this super-philosophical content is no less strict in the East, and is frequently stricter, than in the case of our medieval scholastic systems, which were dependent on the Christian revelation and on the dogmas and ritual of Catholic tradition.

We should not, however, be misled by this into inferring that the category "religion" is more suited than "philosophy" to define our object. Again, the East also certainly has "religions," but with reference to the aspects that are of interest to us, we must understand that the word "religion" often designates widely different things. We, in the West, conceive of religion as a theistic system based on the notion of a personal God, and of the relations between God and man as those of the Creator with His creature, leaving an ontological hiatus between the two. Faith, worship, revelation, divine grace, dogma, and redemption complete the picture which the word "religion" brings before our minds. As a matter of fact, all this is only pertinent to a particular *type* of religion, by which, however, many presume to measure every religious form, pre-Christian (in the case of Europe) as well as Oriental.

Here, again, we should consider the possibility of a "break in level" which would give access to a higher sphere. This sphere is defined by the doctrine of the "Supreme Identity" (not to be mistaken for some form of pantheism); or by a concept of the Absolute ranking high above the theistic idea; or, again, by the overcoming of the creation conception and of the path of faith by means of the principles of pure knowledge and spiritual awakening. Even though some glimmer of these wider and freer horizons has been caught here and there in the Christian West, the premises for a grasp of their real nature have been lacking, nor has their transcendence beyond the world of religion been clearly realized.

On this subject many may perhaps be induced to utilize the category of "mysticism," which again would lead us astray. If by "mysticism" we mean direct experience as against more dogmatic theological speculation, we may accept the term. "Mysticism" is also acceptable as a classification if, tracing it back to its origin, we think of the Mysteries of Antiquity which no doubt were off-shoots of the one universal tradition in the West. But if we use the word in its ordinary modern sense, we must dismiss it as the expression of a confusingly indefinite something based on a fusion of irrational, visionary, and ecstatic emotions from which the intellectual element, clear perception, and knowledge are missing. This is why mystics appear as isolated individuals, one might say as "*Einzelgänger*," who have by chance broken through one or another gate without forming any "chain," without having been shaped by a common tradition, and without being endowed with that superior knowledge which would allow them to grasp the inner significance of their personal achievements. It is possible to reach out beyond these limits, because there exist paths sanctified by tradition and age-old experience for the fulfilment of Nietzsche's precept "Man is something that must be transcended," and for the attainment of knowledge of what the ancient West called the "super-world" and conceived in terms of Olympian clarity. To all this the East we have in mind can bear witness.

Two further aspects of the currents still treasured by Oriental tradition may here be noted, firstly, the sharp differentiation of real spirituality, to be essentially defined in terms of knowledge, of *gnosis,* from all things pertaining to morality and ethics; secondly just the opposite of that fancied "Asiatic contemplative inertia" of which many Westerners speak with a contempt only equaled by their ignorance. According to the Oriental teaching to which we are referring, spiritual knowledge and awakening are always connected with "power"

as their natural consequence—power over both nature and men.

At last the magic circle of Western "humanism" is broken by the general view of life afforded by the Traditional East. This view widens all spiritual horizons; earthly birth is no longer considered as the beginning of conscious being, just as death is no longer deemed to be a significant and tragic event, beyond which there is either a void, or the vague foreshadowings of religious mythology. Through such an outlook transcendence can be brought within the framework of immanence, so that reality is not escaped but transfigured, the one being completed by the other. Such is the East; and it recalls a reality once known also to the West, even though less intensely and universally before secularization and rationalism got the better of it.

If accepted in an undiluted form, and disassociated from esoteric and idiosyncratic elements, these lines of thought might exert an unequaled liberating power. But it is a destructive power as well if we consider the conventional values prevailing in present-day civilization and culture: speculation, conventional religious sentiment, vague mysticism, and the general conception of life based exclusively on "the human condition." All this, when compared to the horizon to which we have referred, is brought to a crisis, and shows itself as problematic and devoid of absolute value. Did not the Katha Upanishad warn that the pathway to knowledge is like a razor's edge? And did not the tradition of the Far East advise us not to follow the Dragon in its flights above the clouds?

Now, just on this point we sense a highly significant convergence, because, as we have pointed out, this crisis, this relativization is also coming about within the present-day civilization of the West as the inevitable consequence of forces and processes which are set irrevocably in motion, and are in the nature of the terminal phase of a cycle. Now the insertion of the above mentioned spiritual values of the East at this very point may produce the effect that dissolution may lead to purification and liberation, and that we may pass beyond destruction straight to an absolute beginning.

"Modern man," wrote C. G. Jung, "may deem himself lucky

because, when he came in contact with the thought and experience of the East, his spiritual poverty was such that he failed
even to perceive the nature of the reality he had come up
against. So he can now restrict his relations with the East to the
innocuous plane of intellectualism, for the rest leaving the matter to Sanskrit scholars."[3] As a matter of fact, these words can be
turned against Jung himself, theories of psychoanalysis having
been responsible for one of the most dangerous misrepresenta-
tions of the Traditional spirituality of the East. Yet he is right in
warning us that contact with the East may be an event of very
different import from what is fancied by vegetarian "spiritualists" or amateur intellectuals. The point of contact, as we have
said, reaches down to the depths; it lies in the path not of those
who in the West become confused, draw back, and try to resist,
but of those who are not afraid of forging on to extremes. The
latter in most cases hurl themselves blindly forward, fight in the
dark, and do not know what is to come thereafter. They do not
realize that they are clearing the way for the contingent advent
of a new cycle beyond the modern world as a whole.[4] Now this
is just the sort of situation in which a knowledge of Oriental spirituality may act substantively.

We are not going to inquire here into the specific forms in
which this influence may he brought to bear on situations not
on the planes of knowledge and action. Some allusion to the
subject has already been made in my article on a special current
of Hindu thought, Tantrism, published in this periodical.[5] Here

---

[3] C. G. Jung, *Psychologie und Alchemie* (Zurich: Rascher, 1944), p. 484;
Psychology and Alchemy, trans. R. F. C. Hull (New York: Pantheon
Books, 1952).

[4] It may be pointed out that the "cycles" doctrine offers an example
of cases where things confusedly foreshadowed by individual Western
thinkers might be integrated by notions of a Traditional effective
knowledge well-known in the East.

[5] See Chapter 2 below. Some other aspects of this question have
been considered in our work *Ride the Tiger* to be published shortly [Jul-

we have dealt with the general aspects, and we can sum up our views as follows. Firstly, the starting point should be the recognition of a spiritual heritage, which preceded, and is superior to, the East-West antithesis. In one particular sector, this finds its counterpart also on the historical and empirical plane, through the fundamentally common origin of the great Indo-European civilizations.

In the second place, we must morphologically single out a type of civilization which, like the modern one, is exclusively based on human conditions, and we must oppose to it a spiritual trend based on real and regular contact with a transcendent reality. Finally, as regards the practical problem, the possibility of a "return" conditioned by conversion should be considered: that which is now making itself felt at the close of a historic cycle through crises of many kinds and confused efforts at liberation may, if a suitable change or reversal of the polarity is made, lead to a new manifestation of what existed at the beginning and was lost. And it is in the East more than elsewhere, in the still uncorrupted East not yet caught up in the vortex of the modern world, that superhuman spirituality and a knowledge of the origins is still to a considerable extent preserved, while the West is standing on that edge for which Goethe's words "*Stirb und werde*"[6] are valid. It will be, therefore, a question of the utmost importance whether the East, now rushing at a disconcerting pace towards a stormy and chaotic period, will be able to resist spiritually and hold its ground till the moment when an effective contact between it and the West can be established. From this point of view, the problem of the future relations between East and West is seen to acquire universal significance, over and above the respective interests of either of the two civilizations.

East & West, vol. 2, no. 1 (April 1951): pp. 23–27

---

ius Evola, *Ride the Tiger: A Survival Manual for the Aristocrats of the Soul*, trans. Joscelyn Godwin and Constance Fontana (Rochester, Vt.: Inner Traditions, 2003)].

[6] "Die and become," from Goethe's poem "Selige Sehnsucht" ("Blissful Yearning"). —Eds.

WHAT TANTRISM MEANS TO MODERN WESTERN CIVILIZATION

One of the characteristics of the Hindu doctrine that may be described in a general way as Tantrism is its claim to offer a formulation of the Traditional doctrine that is only suitable to the last epoch of the present cycle, i.e., for the Kali Yuga. Notwithstanding its importance, it was little known in the West up until a short time ago. It is said that teachings, rituals, sciences, which might have been suitable during the primordial age (Satya Yuga) are no longer suitable for a humanity living in later epochs, especially in the "dark age."

Therefore, such a humanity can find, not in the Vedas or in other ancient texts, but in the Tantras and the Agamas, the knowledge and the techniques allowing it to attain the supreme goal of man: freedom from every form of conditional existence. Thus the Tantras often present themselves as a "fifth Veda" — as a further revelation corresponding to the present phase of manifestation. They further state that former rituals have become as inefficient as "a snake deprived of its venom" inasmuch as the prevailing capability (*adhikara*) in man has undergone a complete change.[1]

However, such a point of view is not valid just in the spiritual "space" of Hindu civilization and tradition, because the doctrine of the four ages has, so to speak, a general validity. There are Western doctrines that correspond to the Hindu formulation of this doctrine. It is in fact sufficiently clear that the last phase ("the iron age" in Western terminology) bears all the signs of modern civilization, the center of which is the West.[2]

---

[1] With reference to all this, see for example: Mahanirvana Tantra, I, 19; II, 7, 14; IV, 47; Tarapradipa, 1; Shiva Shiandra: Tantratattava, trans. Arthur Avalon (Sir John Woodroffe), *The Serpent Power: The Secrets of Tantric and Shaktic Yoga* (London: Luzac & Co., 1919).

[2] For comparisons among the various formulations of the doctrine

As things are, one may be led to consider the extent to which the "relevance" claimed by Tantrism has a certain objective basis, particularly regarding Western Civilization.

Historically, Tantrism is connected with a characteristic revolution that began in India towards the middle of the first millennium BC. Since that time, certain divine female figures — Shakti — rise to ever-growing importance, accompanying Hindu deities which in the Aryan period appeared as isolated, and, in several cases, even obtaining an advantage over them. Shaktism is one of the central aspects of Tantrism.

Now, from a metaphysical point of view, the "divine couple" is a symbol of the two primary aspects of every cosmic principle: the male deity representing the unchangeable and transcending aspect and the female one representing power, strength, force of manifestation, and, in a certain sense, also the active and immanent aspect. Therefore, the appearance of Shaktism in the ancient Hindu-Aryan world, apart from its popular and devotional forms, is a barometrical sign of a change in beliefs. It tells us how, compared to the former consciousness of man, which was focused on the realm of being, the "manifestation" and "action" aspects of the deity were felt more directly and took on a special importance.[3]

Now there is no question whether in this we have simultaneously also the basic character of modern Western civilization, in which immanentism is the by-word. Furthermore, the chief meaning of the word Shakti is capacity to act, authority, and power. Speculative Tantrism conceives the world, life, and man as existing essentially as a sort of power. It speaks of an *active* "Brahman." Maya, carried back to Maya-Shakti, no longer

of the four ages and its utilization in the general metaphysics of history, see Julius Evola, *Revolt Against the Modern World*, trans. Guido Stucco (Rochester, Vt.: Inner Traditions, 1995), Part II.

[3] The fact that in certain aspects Shaktism must be considered as a revival of a pre-Aryan archaic substratum does not alter the aforementioned interpretation.

means a cosmic illusion, but rather the manifestation of her essence, which is made up of will, "*icchamayi*."

Moreover, Kali—an equivalent of Shakti, who according to the Tantra "is entirely awake" in the Kali Yuga—also has her demonic, unchained, and savage aspects. Could it not be that their counterpart in the modern world is whatever can cause the irruption of irrational and elemental forces: a "tellurism" and a demon of collectivistic currents which, at bottom, reveal themselves as the soul of the same world of technology? Their counterpart is made up by the religion of the future, by "vitalistic" theories, and by the discovery of the unconscious-instinctive, nocturnal face of the soul.

It cannot be denied that, under this aspect, there are motives in the Tantric conception capable of serving as the mirror of modern civilization in its most daring and problematic forms. On the other hand, what other point of view could be more fascinating for the Westerner's vocation than the one for which, according to Louis de la Vallée Poussin, the Absolute Self ceases to be an ecstatic experience and becomes instead something that he, who has seen the light, can grasp and master.[4]

In the person of the adept, in the Siddha, and in the Vira, the Tantric Kaula exalt the individual who is superior to every pair of contraries, is free from both good and evil, and whose law is only his will (*shvecchacari*), thus going much further that Nietzsche's "superman." By following this road, the asceticism of a mortifying type is replaced by Hatha Yoga techniques that tend to command the inmost forces of the body, together with a wisdom that proclaims, along with Kularnava Tantra: "The body is the temple of God and the living consciousness (*jiva*) is the eternal Shiva (*Sadashiva*)."

The ritual Tantric secret (*pancatattva*) proclaims the non-existence of the antithesis between asceticism and enjoyment, between *yoga* and *bhoga*. It promises the possession of the one

---

[4] Louis de La Vallée Pouissin, *Bouddhisme: Etude et materiaux* (London: Luzac & Co., 1898), p. 48.

and of the other, pointing out that the place of liberation is in this world and not in the other one (*yoga bhojate, mokshyate samsarah*).

The observance of moral rules as well as of visible rites is, in such circles, declared to pertain only to the *pashu*, to the man bound, obtuse, and resembling an animal, while Tantrism promises the esoteric knowledge that makes one free and breaks all chains.[5]

On the basis of this, one might be tempted to speak of a "modern" and even a "Western" Tantrism. And yet in doing so a misunderstanding would certainly arise. These convergences do not erase a fundamental difference in planes and tendencies. Only by acknowledging this difference would it be possible to admit that Tantrism may lead the way for a Western elite that does not want to become the victim of those experiences whereby an entire civilization is on the verge of being submerged.

Firstly, it is worth stressing the point that in Tantrism the enhancing of forces, truths, and qualifications prevailing in the Kali Yuga neither allows a lower level, nor does it allow the datum of existence to be considered as a last appeal and still less (as in the case of many of our immanent philosophies) as something that must be and must also be glorified.

The values belonging to the highest spiritual realization, such as those of the ancient Hindu metaphysical tradition, are maintained. The actual problem of our age is to find the method to carry them into effect. This method, justly compared to "riding on the back of a tiger," may be summed up in this principle: "In order to obtain freedom, one must employ those same forces that have led to the downfall."

To find the right way in this respect, one must bear in mind that, in the Tantric theory of manifestation, the actual preva-

---

[5] For more on Tantrism, see Julius Evola, *The Yoga of Power: Tantra, Shakti, and the Secret Way*, trans. Guido Stucco (Rochester, Vt.: Inner Traditions, 1992).

lence of the Shaktic element in a given phase (the descending phase, *pravrtti-marga*) does not mean anything when compared to the ratio of metaphysical subordination of the Shakti to the principle opposed to it, Shiva, Purusha, or whatever the male counterpart of the Shakti may be called. In this way some points of reference already exist that are completely missing in the modern views of Western activism, of which, in a certain sense, they are the reverse.

In point of fact, according to Hindu and Tantric views, all action, dynamism, and becoming have a female and negative character. On the contrary, whatever is permanent, unchangeable, and central has a truly male and positive character, possessing the gift of light and being, or, in other words, is the "Lord of the Scepter" (*vajra-dhara*).

This point, therefore, establishes a definite difference between modern horizons and those belonging to the higher forms of Tantrism. If, in the modern world, it is possible to recognize a saturation of the Shaktic element, particularly in its lowest, materialistic, and irrational aspects, the Shivaitic counterpart is lacking. The latter may be termed the true spiritual virility, closely connected to values, tendencies, and sciences even the ideas of which are now lost in the West.

And all this is taken in due consideration by Tantrism, and not in terms of a merely abstract speculation but as a practice. One can thus clearly see what meaning this tendency may have for people who, even if considered as individuals in themselves, want to impose a limit to forces which otherwise would only result in dissolution.

Shakti is the basis of Tantric life, but the method consists in understanding it with an intensity which, in a certain sense, renders it self-consuming and makes of it an instrument of transformation and transfiguration for an objective change to another plane. It must not be forgotten that the main characteristics of Tantric deities should be considered as symbols of destructive forces laid bare, unfettered, superior to all laws. Kali,

Durga, or, in some aspects, Shiva-Rudra himself have such a nature as to be simultaneously the deities of pure transcendence and of internal liberation.

In this connection, a "sacrificial" tendency and a "transforming" moment are to be found in all Tantric methods, even in those that border on magic in a strict sense or on orgiastic revelry—just as a sacred and initiative framing is inseparable from all metaphysics and from the Tantric idea of the world considered as a "power." This again represents a line of separation, and it is easy to understand fully the condition in which the Western ideal of the affirmation of the Self and its freedoms may avoid destructive revolutions, of which we have already certain grim forebodings.

Leaving aside the more exterior and materialistic aspects of the modern civilization of action, it is now necessary to consider what, in a certain sense, may be taken as its central feature. It is the tendency to glorify man, which began during the Renaissance and which, in passing through critical idealism, ethical rationalism, and the "autonomous" morals of the categorical imperative, has arrived at the training of pure willpower and the ideal of the superman.

The basis of this tendency remains, on the whole, on a naturalistic, individualistic, and intellectual plane. In such a way, it ends in a blind alley. If we consider it seriously, it is equivalent to a saturation of strength which, given the limitations of human nature, can only end in a short circuit, in the collapse of the superman into the demonic or into forms of spiritual gymnastics, already condemned by ancient wisdom as a dangerous deviation from true spiritual realization.

In the West, where one hesitates before the advance of these dire consequences, many believe that the only solution is to give up and to allow religion, in its mystical/humanitarian aspects, and an ethic of forgiveness, to come to the fore.

But all of the other initiatic teachings, even Western ones, Yoga in general, and Tantric and Vajrayanic Yoga in particular, tells us that this alternative may be overcome and that a clear path actually exists, even if according to the saying of the Katha Upanishad it is like walking on a razor's edge. What the West needs to learn here is that it is a question of an essential and ontological change in nature.

To speak of a "superman" may lead to a misunderstanding. The Western superman expresses the extreme limit or potentiality of the human species, while in Yoga it is the bridge from one species to another, and, as a goal, it is the detachment from every conditional state, be it human or divine, that one strives to reach through a positive technique confirmed by a multimillennial tradition, a state that has nothing in common with a demonic state of the intellect and with the prevarications peculiar to the religion of materialistic man.

It is therefore obvious to see where the present road ends and a new one begins. In specific reference to Tantra, there are tendencies in common with the Western desire to realize an independent and sovereign will.

But, in Tantra this desire no longer appears as "Luciferian" or "titanic," but, one might say, as "Olympian" — if one bears in mind the same Tantric symbolism according to which the Shakti embraces the impassive "divine male" made of light and bearing a scepter, and to whom she is the raiment of power.

Second, in following this course it is necessary *to do things with sincerity*. An exceptional qualification is required. Carefulness and an intense concentration are necessary, and these have nothing in common with the ideas of the philosophies of immanence and voluntarism, nor with any common mental attitudes.

Third, one must forsake the illusions and pride of the individual self, of what in Hindu terms might be called the Samsaric Self or the Self of elements (*Bhutatma*) which is practically the only one known to the great majority of modern Westerners. In fact the *destruction* of this Self is the condition of true freedom and true power, so that it is the aim of a good number of Yogic techniques as well as of the Tantric ones, even if they are of a Dionysian or orgiastic character.

All this that pertains to the Kali Yuga must be kept in mind by every Westerner who, although remaining in the same trends in which the predominant forces of his civilization have developed, desires once more by virile means to pave the way towards the higher spheres which he had forsaken under the pretext of "conquering the world."

Other factors must also be taken into consideration in order that illusions may not arise, and that the contribution of Hindu spirituality of the Yoga type may be clearly understood.

As already hinted, Tantrism follows above all the way of Hatha Yoga, and this also appears to coincide with modern Western tendencies, because contempt for the body is replaced by the ideal of complete mastery over it. But this mastery is *internal*. In spite of the lack of comprehension due to certain publications divulged in the West, it has nothing of a physical or physiological character.

But the Tantric ways leading to the body and originating from the interior, from the "subtle" body, and along the lines of which supernormal experiences may develop, present great difficulties for the majority of Westerners on account of internal, centuries-old processes having taken on almost a constitutional character. To modern man the inner side of the body is closed to him in the same way in which the non-physical, non-sensible, non-spatio-temporal aspects of the external world are closed. Yoga points the Westerner on the way to be followed so that his soul may master the body and — in accordance with the same ancient Western theory of the relation between macrocosm and microcosm — discover in the body, thus mastered and rendered conscious, the source of unusual powers. It remains, however, to be seen in what measure we may follow this way and acquire a real knowledge of these processes.

The last point to be taken in consideration, particularly because it is generally misunderstood in Western publications, is that it would be difficult to neglect, in realizations of this kind, the transmission of given "influences" of a spiritual and super-individual character brought about by established forms of initiation. Just as the short-circuits mentioned above may be caused by immanentism and modern willfulness one must also point out the difficulty for the individual in surpassing himself, unless exceptional cases are taken into consideration, as compared to the whims of a deceptive self-affirmation. We should remember how the greatest European scholar of Tantrism, Sir John Woodroffe, told us that he could not accept the conditions required of him in order to enter into relations with Tantric initiatic organizations, of anything more than simple, doctrinal acceptance.

In conclusion, what we have stressed before is hereby confirmed. On the one side there is thus a correspondence between some fundamental Tantric ideas and some predominant tendencies of the modern spirit, on account of which one can notice a certain basis in Tantra's claim to present a teaching suitable to the last age, i.e., to the present day. On the other hand, a well-defined line of demarcation exists between the two domains, in the exposition of which we have spared no effort.

The capability of certain specially-qualified Western minds to cross this line corresponds to the measure in which one can remain faithful to the principal way followed by our civilization without thereby being led towards a crisis without resolution. They could change, at least on their own account, a strong poison into a healing medicine. The force that causes some to fall, causes in others a resurrection and participation in something supreme and shining, beyond those powers without center and scope that belong to the dark age.

East & West, vol. 1, no. 1 (April 1950): pp. 28–32

THE *SVADHARMA* DOCTRINE
& EXISTENTIALISM

In an earlier essay I pointed out the importance of clarifying the points at which a connection emerges between the doctrines of the Traditional East and certain very advanced intellectual trends of the West. I then said that in many cases a serious and non-amateurish knowledge of the former might well serve to *complete* the latter, liberating them from their aspect as mere opinions of a purely individual and speculative nature, and also from everything affected by an atmosphere of crisis, such indeed as is that of our own modern, Western civilization. In this way it would be possible to rise from those vague intuitions, attained by Europeans who are struggling in a state of profound critical labor, to the plane of an objective and superpersonal knowledge, which should be defined as *wisdom* rather than as "love of wisdom" (philosophy).

I here wish to deal in this manner with certain specific aspects of a trend of thought, very fashionable today, known as "existentialism," selecting as a counterpart to it the Hindu doctrine of "*svadharma.*"

With reference to existentialism I shall naturally not consider its eccentric and bohemian forms, of a predominantly literary character, which are unfortunately those to which this trend chiefly owes its new popularity. I wish rather to refer to the serious, philosophical existentialism, which took shape well before the Second World War, and which, after Søren Kierkegaard (and in certain respects Nietzsche), had as its chief interpreters Jaspers, Heidegger, and Barth. I will first try to set forth certain basic ideas of existentialism in the most accessible manner. This task is no easy one in a short article, on account of the peculiar, almost esoteric nature of the terminology of the existentialists, in which many words are often used with meanings wholly different from their usual ones.

The basis of existentialism lies in the concept of "existence."

Now, this term must not be taken in the common, ordinary sense. Existence, according to Kierkegaard, signifies the paradoxical and contradictory point in which the finite and the infinite, the temporal and the eternal are implicated and meet. For "existence" here is naturally meant that of the Ego, of the individual being, which is consequently considered to be a synthesis of contradictory elements. His spiritual situation is such that he cannot affirm himself (the finite being who exists in time), without also affirming the "other" than himself (the unconditioned, the atemporal,[1] the absolute being); but, on the other hand, he cannot affirm the transcendent without also affirming himself, the being existing in time. To doubt the one means also to doubt the other. This is the general premise of existentialism, as asserted by all its leading interpreters, from Kierkegaard to Lavelle, from Barth to Jaspers.

Here it is suitable to point out the harmony of this line of thought with the views of Traditional Hinduism. In the first place, there is the question of method: existentialism seeks to reach an intimacy in the very center of the individual, which should at the same time have the value of metaphysical experience. But this may be said to be the method of the whole of Upanishadic Yoga and also Buddhist philosophy, to which we may well apply the formula of a "transcendental experimentalism." In the second place, it is obvious that this ambiguous meeting point between the center of the finite being and the unconditioned more or less reminds us of the *atma*, which presents the actual features, so to speak, of an "immanent transcendency," of something which is the Ego, and at the same time a super-Ego, the eternal Brahman.

Nevertheless the paradox of "existence," understood in the above-mentioned sense, takes the form of a dilemma. We find ourselves, as it were, before an unsustainable position of unstable equilibrium, which must be resolved in the function of one or the other of the two terms, which meet in the individual, but seem to exclude, to contradict each other as well: the conditioned

---

[1] Here the translation has "temporary," but from the context we infer that the opposite sense is correct. — Eds.

and the unconditioned, the temporal and the non-temporal.

The two possible solutions correspond to two directions actually followed by existentialism, in connection with which I may mention the names of Heidegger and Sartre on the one hand, and of Jaspers and above all Barth on the other.

The solution proper to Heidegger's philosophy is that of the man who tries to find the unconditioned in the transitory. The answer, according to this thinker, presents itself as follows: existence in time means existing as an individual and as an individualized being. But individuality signifies particularity; it signifies the affirmation and assumption of a certain group of possibilities, to the exclusion of others, the whole of the others; but these subsist, they live within the individual, they constitute the sense of the infinite within him, and tend to find expression, to realize themselves. This determines the movement of the Ego in time, a movement conceived in the sense of emerging from ourselves (from our own defined particularity), as a tendency to realize all that which we have excluded from ourselves, to live through it in a succession of experiences: a succession which evolves as does time, and which should represent the substitute for totality, for all that which the individual, as such, cannot be at one and the same time. Naturally, to the infinitude of possibilities corresponds necessarily the infinitude of time, and all this gives to some extent the feeling of pursuing one's own shadow: a pursuit without ever attaining, without ever entirely gaining possession of oneself, so as to calm and solve the antithesis and the *angst* proper to "existence."

This solution of Heidegger's thus ends in a sort of metaphysical justification or sanctification of that which, in Hindu terms, might be called *samsara*, the *samsaric* consciousness. This seems to us a dangerous position, inasmuch as it veers towards the various modern Western philosophies of immanency, of "Life," of becoming, a position which, in our opinion, can only with difficulty be linked with any Traditional conception of the world. Indeed, an unconcealed gloomy pessimism broods over the whole of Heidegger's philosophy.

The second existentialist trend, that of Jaspers and Barth, is in a different situation. Starting from more or less similar premises, importance is given to the concept that, if the individual represents one particular possibility amid an infinity of others, which fall outside him, this definite possibility emanates from choice. This choice naturally brings us to something which is before time and before existence within time. The solution of the antithesis is given by the "ethics of fidelity": that which we are in time we must assume, we must regard "our own essence as identical to our own existence," if we are to remain true to what we are, having the presentiment that it is something eternal, which, through ourselves, becomes "temporalized" itself; that everything which appears as necessity, as fate, as hardship, points us to something which is *willed*, to a being which is so because he has *chosen* to be so, taking on this particular nature, excluding every other possible nature.

Thus, together with the precept of faithfulness to ourselves, there is, in existentialism, also the precept of clarification (*Erhellung*). The rule of life of this existentialism is not the search for something else, the dispersion of ourselves in the infinite, problematic multiplicity of the perspectives presenting themselves in the outer world, and still less does it signify the pursuit in time—as Heidegger claims—of the mirage of the ever-escaping unconditioned. We should instead assume our own perspective or vision of the world, seize and realize its *meaning*, which is equivalent to saying its transcendental root: that *will* whereby I am what I am. In existence we may realize anything only on the basis of its traces, of its effects. Then existence will appear to be merely the unfolding in time of something which exists before time, and every necessity or finitude will reveal itself as the consequence of the primordial act of a free power.

Whoever knows the doctrine of *dharma* and of *svadharma* cannot fail to note the analogies between it and these existentialist views. According to the Hindu conception, every human being has a nature of his own. It is not mere chance that we are what we are and not something else. To this nature—unless we feel a vocation for a higher ascent—we must remain true; faithfulness to our own nature, whatever it may be, is the highest worship which we may render to the Supreme Spirit.

Thus, to be ourselves is to assume our own position and tend to our own individual perfection, without letting ourselves be distracted or seduced by exterior interests, aims, or values. There is no nature, no *dharma*, superior or inferior to another, if we take—as we should take—the infinite, that which is beyond time, as measure. Hence to betray one's own *dharma*—the law of one's own nature—to assume the *dharma*, the manner of being, the law, the path of another—is error and fault: fault, not in the moral sense, but in the ontological sense. It is a wound against the cosmic order—*Rta*—equivalent to violence against ourselves, because we thus enter into contradiction with ourselves. We wish to be here and now, in time, something different from what we had wished to be outside of time. The effect of this is disintegration, and therefore a descent in the hierarchy of beings (symbolically, a descent into hell).

These are Traditional Hindu concepts which we find expressed in the Laws of Manu, and, in a still more definite form, in the Bhagavad-Gita. We know that in India they have not remained mere theory and philosophy, but have exercised a powerful influence on individual and collective life, constituting, among other things, the ethical and metaphysical basis of the caste system. This system has been little understood by Westerners—although in the Middle Ages they had something of the same kind—and it is about to be cheerfully set aside by the modernized Oriental.

But, the general vision of the world and of man, in which the *svadharma* doctrine is framed, has dimensions which are lacking in existentialism. For this reason it can contextualize and render unexceptionable more than one doubtful point in this Western philosophy.

First of all, we must set aside Barth. He ends up in a theocentrism, which enables him to connect existentialism with Christian theology. This theology, like Thomism, defended the theory of "one's own nature" —*natura propria*—and the ethics of fidelity to that nature, which is different in each man and is willed by God. But here, in our opinion, we are rising too high, and the reference to the divinity, whose will is responsible for being in this or that particular manner, is too facile and convenient an explanation. From the theistic standpoint, the existentialist problem is solved only by faith, by trust in God—even with the promise of a future vision of all things, and consequently also of ourselves, of the course of one own life, "*sub specie aeternitatis*"; a vision through which all obscurity will disappear. But all this is religion rather than metaphysics, and cannot prove satisfactory to all.

Let us then return to Jaspers. The defective points of his theories, in which Hindu ideas can be helpful, concern the nature of that "choice" which must have been made on the non-temporal plane, and which enables us to explain the coexistence, within existence, of the finite and the infinite. Above all the *place* of this choice remains wholly obscure—not less so than in Kant and Schopenhauer, who had already formulated something of the kind with their theories of the "intelligible character."

That obscurity is inevitable, owing to the practical non-existence, in both Western philosophy and religion, of the doctrine of *pre-existence* and of *multiple states of being*. That, before birth, existed not simply the will of God, creating at His good pleasure souls out of nothing; that instead there had pre-existed a certain consciousness-entity, of which the existence of each one of us on earth is the manifestation. All this is "*terra incognita*" for the majority of Western philosophers and theologians; they hardly know anything of this kind.

But without references of this sort, the whole existentialist theory suffers from an initial and basic obscurity. Incidentally it should be noticed that we have spoken of the theory of pre-existence, and not that of "reincarnation" or *karma*, such as Theosophists have disseminated from the end of the last century in certain Western Spiritualist circles. The first theory has nothing to do with the second—the one has a metaphysical, the other a popular character—and, as I have explained on various occasions, taken literally reincarnation explains nothing; indeed it is an error.

From the first fault the second is derived, which refers to the sense of the act whereby we have wished to be what we do indeed find ourselves to be on earth and in time: namely, the sense of transcendent choice or election, which takes the place of the Divine will and which is also a necessary precondition of being able to speak of responsibility, and of justifying the principle of fidelity to our true nature.

Now, in this Jaspers only sees a defect: to have wished to be individuals signifies having wished to limit ourselves. But to limit ourselves signifies sin—sin against the infinite, against the unconditioned, which is fatally denied in all possibilities, in all manners of being excluded from the horizon of that single definite life. And sin is naturally associated with anguish, the famous "existential angst" of the Ego.

This is indeed a strange idea, which betrays a certain pessimism, of which we find traces in the earliest Greek philosophy and even in Orphism. If at the beginning of things, up on high, on the hither side of time, there has truly been a free power, we cannot understand what "defect," what "sin" there can have been for him to have made a choice, for having decided in favor of one mode of existence and not another. That other possibilities must thereby have been excluded or denied, is simply logical and inevitable—nor do we know to whom the bearer of that freedom should answer.

In any case, to speak here of "sin" is really nonsense. Should we regard as a sin (generating existential angst) the fact that, having a free evening, I elect to spend it in a nightclub—which of course prevents me from doing other things, such as going to a theatre, or to a lecture, or remaining at home to study, and so on?

The true infinite for us, and for every true metaphysics, is not that which is, so to speak, condemned to ecstatic and indeterminate infinity. *It is that which it is*, which it wishes to be, remaining unconditioned in its every act, retaining the sense of its primordial freedom and unconditioned state in all which it has willed and in which it has become. Once we have entered into the dominion of temporality, we must bear in mind that which they call in the Far East the law of concordant action and reaction, and which the Hindus call *karma*, but in its true sense, not in that of the Theosophists and popularizers.

It would be sufficient to enter into this order of ideas to confer on the above-mentioned existentialist notions an entirely different meaning, to remove from them everything connected with "crisis," "angst," "invocation," or dispersion in a petty, arbitrary "choice." All would pass on to a plane of higher calm, transparency, and decision. And the principle of being true to ourselves, of fidelity to our being to the "place" we have in the reign of temporality, would acquire illumination—thanks to its relation with a truly unconditioned and super-individual order.

Indeed, the corresponding Hindu view—which the ancient West already knew (Plotinus, for instance, and even Plato before him)—might act in this sense on the existentialists who might then really live their own problems. And this would be the most significant point of a possible encounter between the thought of the Traditional East, and that of the contemporary West.

Note

On the doctrine of *dharma* and castes, see my book *Revolt Against the Modern World,* Part I, Chapter 14.

East & West, vol. 3, no. 3 (October 1955): pp. 168–71

RENÉ GUÉNON:
EAST & WEST

The new edition of René Guénon's *The Crisis of the Modern World* offers the opportunity for a critical account, which may be of some interest, of the author's major ideas. These ideas are closely connected with the problem of the relation between East and West, and of the fate that awaits our civilization as a whole. They are all the more interesting as Guénon dissents from all those who for some time now have been writing about the "decline of the West," the "crisis of the European spirit," and so forth—all ideas which today, after the new collapse brought about by the Second World War, have again come to the fore with renewed vigor.

Guénon does not deal with individual cases and confused reactions, nor does he deal with philosophy in the current sense of the word; his ideas originate from Tradition in a broad and impersonal sense. Unlike the writers alluded to above—Spengler, Ortega y Gasset, Huizinga, Massis, Keyserling, and Benda—Guénon does not belong spiritually to the modern world. He bears witness to a different world, and he makes no mystery of the fact that he owes his knowledge to a great extent to the direct contact he has had with the exponents of the traditional East.

Guénon takes as his starting point—and we believe it is essential and can be accepted without discussion—that the real antithesis is not between East and West, but between Traditional civilization and modern civilization. The antithesis is, therefore, neither geographical nor historical, but of a morphological and typological character.

Indeed, we may describe as "Traditional" a universal type of civilization that has been attained, even if in various forms and more or less completely, both in the East and in the West.

"Traditional" civilizations—all Traditional civilizations—have metaphysical points of reference. They are characterized by the recognition of an order superior to everything human and temporal; and by the presence and the authority exercised by elites who derive from this transcendent plane certain principles and values. These are needed for attaining a higher system of knowledge, as well as for bringing about a social organization based on the recognition of hierarchical principles, and for giving a truly profound meaning to life. In the West, the Middle Ages still offered an example of a Traditional civilization of this type.

Modern civilization, whether Western or Eastern, is the direct opposite of Traditional civilization. It is characterized by the systematic denial of everything superior to man—whether considered as an individual or as a community—and by the organization of unsanctified forms of knowledge, of action, and of life that see nothing beyond temporal and contingent realities; that lead to the reign of quantity, and by logical necessity bear in themselves from the start the germs of all those crises and disorders of which the world now offers such striking and widespread evidence.

In Guénon's opinion, the situation in the East is different. The East still preserves living aspects of "Traditional civilization" that have disappeared elsewhere. Guénon believes that the modern world can only overcome the crisis from which it suffers by a return to a Traditional type of civilization. But this cannot arise from nothing. As the West has long lost touch with its previous Traditional forms, of which—apart from the religious world very narrowly understood—almost nothing remains.

Guénon considers that the contact between the elites of the West and the representatives of the Traditional spirit of the East is a matter of essential importance for securing a revival, for "galvanizing," so to speak, latent forces. It is not a question of being untrue to ourselves by trying to become orientalized. Rather, it is a question of receiving from the East something that can be used in rediscovering our own Tradition and thus rise above the purely human, individualistic, and rationalistic civilization of recent times; to form, little by little, a milieu favorable to the revival of a Traditional West.

At this point, an understanding between East and West would come about naturally and would rest on foundations quite different than those conceived by all who have reflected on such problems from an exclusively political, or abstractly cultural or economic, or vaguely "spiritual," standpoint.

In the abstract, Guénon's ideas seem to us quite acceptable, and he deserves credit for formulating them rigorously, with an uncompromising obedience to truth and truth alone. We must, however, express reservations when we pass from the general to the particular, to the world outlook and the symbols needed for effective action.

If we turn to the East, Guénon's views must be brought up to date, for since the first edition of this book, many things have changed and changed rapidly. It becomes more evident every day that the East itself, understood as representing Traditional civilization, is passing through a crisis. China is no longer in the picture. In India, nationalistic and modernizing trends are steadily gaining ground. The Arab countries and even Tibet are in confusion. Thus, much of Guénon's East seems to be becoming a thing of the past, and those parts of the East where the Traditional spirit still survives, thanks to uninterrupted continuity, and which might fulfill the function to which we have already referred, are to be found, if at all, in some small and rather exclusive groups of select spirits, destined by the course of events to play an ever smaller part in the historical destinies of their peoples. It is to be hoped that at least these small groups will succeed in remaining immune to the modernizing influences to which most Orientals have unfortunately succumbed, in trying to accommodate one aspect of their civilization to Europe or America. Otherwise the problem, as stated by Guénon, would be deprived of its most important element. As things stand, we must reiterate that the ideas expressed by Guénon might well be received with skepticism should they lead us to seek something that could serve us as a model in the present-day civilization of the East. Nor is there any reason to expect that things will change in the near future.

Now, we should say something about the cyclical laws that play such an important role in traditional teachings and to which Guénon himself makes frequent reference. In contrast to optimistic and progressive Western myths of the seventeenth and eighteenth centuries, those laws speak of a gradual loss of spirituality and of Tradition the further we travel from the point of departure. All the negative and critical features of modern civilization are accounted for by the fact that they correspond to the last phases of a cycle, the phase known in India as the Kali Yuga, the "Dark Age," described many centuries ago in terms that reflect in a striking way the physiognomy of the present-day West.

Indeed, our civilization may well be the epicenter of the "Dark Age." But those laws apply to the East as well, so we cannot exclude the possibility that tomorrow a very special solution to the relations between East and West may be found. As we Westerners advance further along the downward path, we are also nearer to the terminal point of the present cycle, and this means that we are also nearer the new beginning than are other civilizations where Traditional forms still survive. We are justified in thinking that, in obedience to those laws, the East will have to travel along our *Via Crucis* and at an infinitely more rapid rate—just think of China!

The whole problem will thus consist in seeing whether Western forces will succeed in leading us beyond the crisis, beyond the zero point of the cycle. Should this be so, it may well be that the East will stand where the West stands today at a time when the West will already have gone beyond the "Dark Age." The relations between the two will thus be inverted. According to this perspective, all that the East represents—not its elites but its real, present-day civilization as a whole—would then be, in a certain sense, a residuum accounted for by the fact that the East has not reached the same point as the West in the cyclical process.

Therefore, generally speaking, the points of reference with which the East can supply us are of an ideal rather than a real order, and one should not view too optimistically the prospects of obtaining from the East genuinely valid help in resisting forces now at work the world over, and which it would be hard to master other than by "riding the tiger."

If we are to consider the possibility of revivifying the West in a way that might not only save her from catastrophe but even place her at the head of the historical movement when the forces of a new cycle are set in motion, then we must consider a certain matter of principle when examining the specific standpoint taken by Guénon. He believes that one of the causes of the crisis of the modern world is the theoretical and practical denial of the priority of knowledge, contemplation, and pure intellectualism over action.

To be sure, Guénon gives a meaning to these terms that differs greatly from the usual one. He uses them to express spiritual activities related to the transcendent order of those pure metaphysical principles which have always laid the permanent foundations for all sound Tradition. It is also obvious that no objection can be raised to the priority of intellectualism over action, if by action we mean something disordered, unenlightened, and purposeless, dominated exclusively by contingent and material considerations, aiming only at worldly achievements. This is now, in fact, the only form of action modern civilization recognizes and admires.

But the Traditional conception of action is quite different. In Tradition, contemplation — or pure knowledge — and action have always been related, the former to the priestly, the latter to the warrior or royal caste (Brahmin and Kshatriya, to use the Hindu terms). Contemplation is a mark specifically of the religious-priestly, while action signifies the warrior and the king.

Once this is established we must go back to a teaching that Guénon himself refers to on more than one occasion, *viz.* that this duality of dignities did not exist in the beginning; that the two powers merged in an apex that was both royal and sacerdotal. Ancient China, the first Aryan Hindu period, Iran, early Greece, Egypt, early Rome and then Imperial Rome, the Caliphate, and so on, all bear witness to this. It is as the result of regression and degeneration that the two dignities separated — and not infrequently were even in strife, as the effect of reciprocal disavowal.

But if this is so, then neither of the two poles can claim absolute priority over the other. Both alike arise from, and have strayed far from, the original ideal and purely Traditional state. And if we were to aim in some way at the restoration of that apex, neither the priestly-contemplative nor the warrior-active could be taken as the foundation stone and starting point. Here, of course, action should not be understood in the modern but in the Traditional sense, in that of the Bhagavad-Gita, or the Islamic *jihad*, or the ascetic orders of chivalry of the Western Middle Ages.

Guénon's own personal inclinations have prevented him from giving adequate recognition to all this, and have led him to attribute exclusive importance to the point of view of action subordinated to contemplation. And this one-sided point of view is not without consequences for the problem of the possible revival of the West.

There can be no doubt that the Western world and Western man are characterized by the priority given to action; Guénon himself admits this. Now if Tradition in its universal sense is one in its metaphysical non-human essence, it admits nevertheless various forms corresponding to the diverse aptitudes and dominant characteristics of the peoples and societies it serves. Now, in the first place, Guénon fails to explain his assertion that the only form of Tradition that was acceptable to the West was religious in character — that is to say directed toward contemplation as its ideal. But the specific character of Westerners is more inclined to action, and in the absence of a Tradition that transfigured and integrated the ideals of action, they have degraded action to the materialistic and savage expressions known to us all. Moreover, prior to Christianity the West had traditions of a different type, and the civilization of the Middle Ages was not one dominated only by the ideas of knowledge and contemplation. We need only call to mind the important Ghibelline expressions of that civilization, even now so little understood in their authentic grandeur and in their deepest significance.

If we consider the future — i.e., the possibility of a revival of the West on Traditional lines — the same question arises. If the West is inclined to action, then action should be the starting point, and one should beware of stigmatizing as heretical and anti-Traditional all that is not based on the premise of the priority of contemplation and knowledge over action. One should instead study forms of civilization which — though Traditional, and giving importance to all that has a metaphysical and not exclusively human character—yet have at their base symbols drawn from the world of action. Only a Tradition of this kind could have a real grip on the nations of the West and could provide them with something organic, compatible, and efficacious.

It is strange that in his many references to Eastern civilizations, Guénon practically ignores Japan. This is again the result of his "personal equation," of his lack of sympathy and understanding for civilizations in which the Brahmanical-sacerdotal interpretation of Tradition does not predominate. But it is Japan that until yesterday offered us a most interesting example of a civilization which in externals had been modernized as a means to an end (for purposes of defense) but which in its inner essence was faithful to a millennial tradition that belonged to the kingly and warrior, and not to the contemplative type. The Samurai caste was its backbone, a caste in which the symbols of action did not exclude but rather postulated elements of a sacred and sometimes even initiatic character. With all the many differences that divide them, that pattern of civilization had discernible similarities to that of the Holy Roman Empire. And there can be no doubt that if Western man were to revive for himself a higher, Traditional vocation, ideals of this kind—duly adjusted and purified—would appeal to him much more than those of the contemplative and purely noetic type.

Guénon uses the expression *élite intellectuelle* in referring to those in the West who should organize—either independently or in collaboration with exponents of the still traditional East—and gradually bring about a change in cultural outlook; to halt the process of dissolution before it completes its fatal and irrevocable progress throughout the whole of the modern world.

As we have said, Guénon does not use the expression "intellectualism" in its generally accepted meaning; those to whom he refers are not "intellectuals," but men of superior character whose formation has been on Traditional lines and who possess a knowledge of metaphysics. Moreover, he mentions an invisible and imponderable form of "indirect action" that such elites can exercise. (Here we might call to mind some of the secret societies of the Chinese, perhaps even the action of Freemasonry in the seventeenth and eighteenth centuries.)

But for all this, the notion of an *élite intellectuelle* gives one the impression of something abstract. If we accept the earlier account of an active and more Western expression of the Traditional spirit, then the idea of an *Order*—analogous to the Templars, Ishmaelites, and Teutonic Knights of old—seems better suited to the purpose than an *élite intellectuelle*. An Order represents a superior form of life within the framework of a life of action, which may have a metaphysical and Traditional "dimension" while at the same time remaining more directly involved with the real world of historical facts.

But all this implies a change of mental outlook, a new vision of the world, which should exercise its influence in all fields of modern culture, including the so-called exact sciences. Now in the case of this more general task, the reservations we have made no longer hold good: all that Guénon says is of undoubted value. He points to the essential principles that must be respected both in recognizing the real nature of the crisis of the modern world, and for laying down the foundations of a return to "integral Traditionalism." His suggestions differ markedly from the scanty proposals now brought forward by those Westerners here and there who have a knee-jerk reaction against the prevailing state of affairs, which they see, more or less clearly, as headed for disaster.

The fact that a Westerner like René Guénon has reached these conclusions through close contact with the authentic exponents of a still Traditional East, rather than by relying solely on his own forces and potentialities, is a fact which has particular significance for us and deserves to be emphasized in these pages.

East & West, vol. 4, no. 4 (1954): pp. 255–58

EAST & WEST:
THE GORDIAN KNOT

The name of Ernst Jünger has now achieved a certain almost Europe-wide notoriety. However, the importance of this writer as a philosopher concerns above all the early period of his activities. An ex-serviceman in the First World War, he appeared as a spokesman of what in his day was already known as the "burnt-out generation." His ideas were drawn not from abstract armchair speculations, but from a heroic experience through which he had lived, from whence they gradually extended to the problem of the meaning of the human person in an epoch of nihilism and the all-powerful machine. His watchwords were those of "heroic realism" and the ethics of the "absolute person."

Unfortunately, Jünger's later production, while it registered an apparent progress from the point of view of pure literature and style, showed a perceptible decline of level and of tension from the standpoint of worldview. A somewhat suspect humanist tendency, associated with myths which by reaction have become fashionable in certain circles even in Central Europe, after the recent collapse, has somehow influenced his later writing.

We have had occasion to peruse a recently-published book of Jünger's entitled *The Gordian Knot* (*Der gordische Knoten*, Frankfurt a.M., 1953). It professes to deal with relations between East and West, regarded as a basic historical theme, with the encounters which have taken place between Europe and Asia from the days of the Persian wars to the present time.

It is not easy to circumscribe the domain considered by Jünger. It hovers essentially between politics and ethics, while the religious and purely intellectual element is almost overlooked. This fact proves prejudicial to the whole work, because, if we do not consider this element as the fundamental background of traditional Oriental civilizations, the whole problem appears badly posed. In this book we find a number of interesting observations, but they are scattered about here and there as if in a conversation, and there is a lack of systematic unity.

However, the fundamental defect of the book is that it presents in terms of historical antitheses and of antithetical civilizations what are instead antitheses of universal spiritual categories, having no necessary relations with particular peoples, civilizations, or continents. Jünger often finds himself forced to admit this, as when he speaks of East and West, of Europe and Asia, not as of two historical and geographical concepts, but as two possibilities which every man in every age carries within himself. Every people would indeed possess them, because, for instance, the typical characteristics of Asiatic incursions into Europe and of the "Oriental" manner of warfare would reappear in civil wars as opposed to regular wars.

But how can we then fail to notice that the greater part of the author's considerations, which resort to historical and geographical references, are compromised by a fundamental one-sidedness and ambiguity? They should instead limit themselves to the domain of a morphology or a typology of civilizations and of world outlooks, and which claim actually to conclude with a diagnosis of the present situation.

That this is the case can be easily proved if we examine some of the main motifs of the book—first of all the one from which the book's very title is drawn, i.e., the Gordian knot. The Gordian knot ought to represent the problem which always arises with every encounter between Asia and Europe when domination over the world is in question.

The Gordian knot represents Asia, while the sword that cuts it represents Alexander's Europe. The former should be the symbol of destiny, of an existence bound by elementary or divine forces, of a world characterized by a lack of limits, of a political society essentially despotic and arbitrary. The sword of Alexander should instead represent the luminous element or spiritual power, and be the symbol of a world acknowledging freedom, law, human respect—a greatness which cannot be reduced to mere power.

At one point in the book the antithesis is even made equivalent to that between the Titanic powers, vast and shapeless, and the Olympian powers eternally opposing them, because the former also represent the substratum of elementary forces ever re-emerging from the depths and offering possibilities for new triumphs and further progress.

We need only bear this formulation in mind to realize the absurdity of talking about "East and West." In fact, this myth of antagonism is invested with a universal character: it is found in the mythologies and sagas of *all* civilizations, and in the East it has been formulated no less distinctly than in Hellenic civilization. (We need only remember the dualism of Mazdaism, the Hindu theme of the struggle between *deva* and *asûra*, or the exploits of Indra, etc.) It reflects, therefore, a vision of life by no means specifically European.

Moreover, if we refer to the metaphysical plane, it is quite absurd to associate the East with an existence subject to the powers of destiny and of the earth. If there is a civilization which has not only formulated the notion of an absolute freedom, of a freedom so high that even the realms of heaven and pure Being appear as forms of bondage, but which has furthermore established a definite praxis in order to realize that ideal, such a civilization is definitely that of the East.

But Jünger seems to wish to keep to a more conditioned plane, closer also to that of political forces. Here too the argument does not hold water. The antithesis of the Western ideal of political freedom as against Asian despotism is an old story, which may have been a "myth" dear to certain Hellenic historians, but which is devoid of all real foundation.

To justify it we would have to limit ourselves to considering certain inferior by-products of a degenerating and barbarous East, with local satraps and despots, with hordes of Tartars, Huns, and Mongols, and some aspects of the latest Arabo-Iranian and Arabo-Persian cycles. At the same time, we would have to overlook recurrent phenomena of the same kind in the West, including the methods of those tyrants and princes of the Italian Renaissance who were devoid of all humanity.

Indeed, Jünger himself counters his own thesis when he points out that in the evolution of Roman history, especially during the Imperial period, both forms were present. He fully realizes that it is not possible here to suggest a remote Asiatic racial contribution as the only workable explanation. So he has to resort, as we have seen, not to historic Asia, but rather to an Asia as a permanent possibility latent in everyone.

In any case, coming to modern times, the impossibility of sensibly utilizing this antithesis in any way appears ever more obvious to Jünger himself. Here his antithesis on the one hand almost identifies itself with that proper to the political terminology of today, in which the "West" is identified with the Euro-American democratic world and the "East" with Bolshevik Russia. In addition, with regard to certain features drawn by him from the "Asiatic" style—concerning the manner of waging war, of estimating the individual, of despotism, of exploiting vanquished peoples and prisoners of war, of wholesale slaughter, etc.—he tends to perceive them, in a rather one-sided manner, in Hitler's Germany. What can all this mean?

In any case, in this connection things are clearly not quite right, and it is odd that Jünger has not noticed it. Leaving Asia and Europe aside and considering instead these conceptions in themselves, the true synthesis does not lie between freedom and tyranny but rather between individualism and the principle of authority. Everything like tyranny, despotism, Bonapartism, the dictatorship of tribunes of the people, is nothing more than a degeneration or an inverted falsification of a system based on the principle of authority.

By reverting to the domain of historical civilizations it would indeed be easy to show to what extent the traditional East, as far as concerns the doctrine of the Regnum, admitted ideals very different from individual despotism. We need only refer to the Far Eastern Imperial conception, with its theory of the "mandate of Heaven" and the strict political ethic of Confucius. In the Niti Sastra we are asked to explain how he who cannot dominate himself (his own *manas*) can dominate other men, and in the Arthashastra the exercise of royal functions is conceived as *tapas*, i.e., ascetism, ascetism of power. We might easily multiply references of this kind.

There is no doubt that the East has had a characteristic tendency toward the Unconditioned, which has been the case only sporadically in the West, by no means to its advantage. This might shed a different light even on what Jünger calls the

Willkürakt,[1] and which in him seems almost to play the part of an angst complex. As a matter of fact, for a world outlook in which the extreme point of reference is the Unconditioned, law in actual practice or in the abstract, can never constitute the extreme instance on any plane, neither the human nor the divine.

We do not wish to dwell here on the evident contradiction into which Jünger falls: how can he reconcile the idea of the East as a world subject to the bonds of destiny and of necessity with that other idea, according to which the absolute act, the *Willkürakt*, is alleged to be an Eastern category? Furthermore, although it is a case of already very different horizons, by such implications we would have to recognize Asia in its purity in, for example, Nietzsche and Stirner.

But it is more important to consider another aspect of the question. Jünger tells of a visit by the Count of Champagne to the head of the Order of the Ishmaelites at the time of the Crusades. At a sign from his host, some knights threw themselves down from the top of a wall. Asked if his own knights were capable of similar obedience and fealty, the Count replied in the negative. We have here, Jünger declares, something which a European mind cannot grasp, because it borders on the absurd, on folly, because it offends all human values. We have the same sentiments toward the Japanese *kamikaze*, devoting themselves to death. Jünger adds that during the Second World War, in Italy and Germany, exploits were conceived and actually carried out which involved extreme risks, but not a prior acceptance of irrevocable sacrifice by the individual.

Now these considerations are one-sided, in part due to misunderstanding. With regard to the first point we shall mention a single instance. Ancient Rome, which certainly did not belong to "Asia," had the ritual of the so-called *devotio*: a military commander volunteered to die as a victim of the infernal powers in order to promote their outbreak and thus to bring about the defeat of the enemy.

The second point, however, is more important. Jünger should have known that the Ishmaelites were not merely a military Or-

---

[1] Arbitrary act. — Eds.

der, but also an Order of initiates. Within the orbit of initiation, all ethics of a merely human nature, however elevated, cease to have any validity. Even on the level of mere religion we find the sacrifice of Isaac as a trial, and a discipline of absolute "corpse-like" obedience — *perinde ac cadaver* according to the formula of the Jesuits — in the domain of monastic asceticism. Calvin went so far as to consider the possibility of renouncing eternal salvation for the sake of the love of God.

As for the Order of the Ishmaelites, a specific point should be borne in mind: absolute obedience to the extreme limit, as illustrated in the above-mentioned episode, also had the value of discipline and was limited to the lower ranks of the initiatic hierarchy; once the individual will is eliminated, above the fourth degree, an absolutely contrary principle reigns, that of absolute freedom, so much so that someone once attributed the principle that "Nothing is true, everything is permitted" to the Ishmaelites.

A mere Crusading knight could hardly attain such horizons: a Templar knight might perhaps have done so, for the Order of the Templars also had an initiatic background. Were Jünger to realize all this he might begin to understand the proper place for what he calls the *Willkürakt* and the limitations of the validity of an ethics of personality, and of an ideal of purely human civic greatness.

Here indeed higher existential dimensions come into play, and not only in the case of an organization of initiates. For instance, when it comes to those "absolute sacrifices" of a heroic nature, we should not forget that in a general way it is a question of civilizations in which human earthly existence is not considered unique and incapable of repetition, as it is with us. Even on the level of popular religion and of the normal outlook on life in those civilizations, the individual has the feeling (or foreboding) that his existence does not begin with birth nor end with death on earth. Thus we find potentially present that consciousness and that higher dimension for which the religious views that have to come to prevail in the West offer a suitable atmosphere only in exceptional cases.

Probably the most important result of these latter considerations is the following. Putting aside East and West, Asia and Europe as civilizations and as historic realities, we may place our consideration on the plane to which Jünger has more than once been forced to shift himself in his book, i.e., on the plane of a morphological determination of the various layers and possibilities of human beings.

We would then have three levels to consider. On the lowest we should place all those possibilities that Jünger has associated with the "Gordian knot," with elementary and savage forces, with everything that is limitless, with the daemonism of destruction, with that which is ruthless, with an absence of all human respect, with affirmation devoid of all law.

In an intermediate zone we should place the sum total of possibilities contained within the framework of a civilization which recognizes the value of *humanitas*, of law, of individual and civic freedom, of culture in the ordinary meaning of the word.

The intermediate level is here represented by that spirituality which Jünger associates with the symbols of Alexander's sword—while the lowest level is made up of the values which have provided the foundations of modern bourgeois and liberal civilization.

But we must recognize as the highest zone that of possibilities which—through the formal analogies which two opposite poles always present—reflect certain features of the first zone, because the highest zone is a domain in which human ties are surpassed; here neither the merely human individual nor the current criterion of human greatness still represent a limit, because within it the Unconditioned and the absolutely transcendent asserts itself. Some of the highest peaks of Oriental spirituality refer, in fact, to this zone. If only a line as narrow as a razor's edge at times separates this domain from the former (since opposition to what is merely human is common to both), still the distance between the two is also like an abyss.

Now it is important to point out that wherever forces belonging to the first of the three domains come forth, only the possibilities open to us in the third domain can really resist them. Any attempt to stem them on the basis of forces and values of the intermediate zone can only be precarious, provisional, and incomplete.

To conclude, we may supplement the above with a remark concerning the diagnosis of the present situation, to which Jünger's book claims to have contributed. In the first phase of his activities, and above all in his books *Feuer und Blut* (1926) and *Der Arbeiter* (1932), he had rightly perceived that the age beginning in the West with the advent of mechanical civilization and of the first "total" war is characterized by the emergence of "elementary" forces operating in a destructive manner—not only materially, but also spiritually; not only in the vicissitudes of warfare, but also in cosmopolitan, mechanized life.

The merit of Jünger in that first phase of his thought is that he had recognized the fatal error of those who think that everything may be brought back to order; that this new menacing world, ever advancing, might be subdued or held back on the basis of the vision of life and the values of the preceding age (i.e., of bourgeois civilization).

If a spiritual catastrophe is to be averted, modern man must make himself capable of developing his own being in a higher dimension—and it is in this connection that Jünger had announced the above-mentioned conception of "heroic realism" and raised up the ideal of the "absolute person." Such a person is capable of measuring himself against elementary forces, capable of seizing the highest meaning of existence in the most destructive experiences, in those actions wherein the human individual no longer counts. Such a man is acclimated to the most extreme temperatures, having passed beyond the "zero point of every value." It is obvious that in all this Jünger had a presentiment of the *metaphysical level of life* characteristic of the third domain we have mentioned.

However, in this new book we see that he confuses this domain with the first, and that the chief points of reference for everything that Jünger associates with the symbol of the West are drawn to a great extent from the intermediate zone—still far enough from the "zero point of every value," and not wholly incompatible with the ideas beloved in the preceding bourgeois period (even if raised to a dignified form and integrated with some of the values of the best of the European tradition).

This leads to a dangerous confusion of horizons, and at all

events marks a retrogression from the positions already achieved by Jünger in his first period. His more recent works, including the one which we have been discussing, while rich in interesting suggestions, offer us nothing of fundamental value.

We have, moreover, seen that in this book on the Gordian knot, the East is a one-sided and partly arbitrary notion which has nothing to do with the actual reality of the higher Traditional Oriental civilizations. While throughout the whole work we perceive with sufficient clarity the reactions of those who, without having any adequate sense of distance, draw conclusions from the most recent political vicissitudes and who would reduce the conflict between East and West merely to that between the world of the democratic Euro-American nations, with their own outworn ideals (which are trying to present themselves in terms of a new European humanism), and the world of Soviet Communism.

East & West, vol. 5, no. 2 (July 1954): pp. 94–98

THE RIGHT TO ONE'S OWN
LIFE IN EAST & WEST

In these brief notes I shall not attempt to deal with the question of the right to life in general, but with the right to one's own life, which corresponds to the ancient formula of *jus vitae necisque*. It is the right to accept human existence, or to put an end to it voluntarily. I intend to compare certain characteristic points of view which have been formulated in this connection in the East and in the West. However, the problem will not be considered from a social point of view, but rather from an interior spiritual one, whence it appears in the shape of a problem of responsibility only to our own selves. For this reason, I shall not deal with theories, such as that of the Japanese *hara-kiri*, or suicide for reasons of honor or loyalty, nor with similar doctrines which we also find in the West.

Perhaps the severest and most virile form in which the right to dispose freely of one's own earthly existence is asserted in the West is found in the theory of Stoicism, and more particularly in the Stoicism of Seneca. This doctrine of suicide, unique on account of the peculiar ethos with which it is justified, may serve for us as a starting point. Seneca and the Roman Stoics conceived earthly existence in the form of a struggle and a test. According to Seneca the real man stands above the gods themselves. The gods, owing to their very nature, do not know adversity and disaster. Man, by contrast, is subject to these, but also has the power of triumphing over them. Unhappy is he who has never encountered disaster and suffering, Seneca wrote, for he has had no occasion to put his own powers to the test and to know them. To man something greater than mere exemption from ills has been granted: the power of triumphing over them within himself. And those beings who have been most subject to trials should be regarded as the worthiest, if we bear in mind that in war the commanders entrust the most exposed positions to the strongest and best qualified men, whereas the less brave, the weaker, and the less trustworthy are employed in the less diffi-cult, but also less glorious positions of the rear.

In a general way, this is also the order of ideas brought for-ward when suicide is condemned and stigmatized as a form of cowardice and desertion. Seneca instead comes to the opposite conclusion, and actually attributes the justification of suicide to God himself (*De Provid.*, VI, 7–9). He makes God say that he has granted to the true man and the wise man a power beyond all contingencies; that he has so disposed things that no one may be restrained when he no longer wishes to be; the way of departure is open to him: *latet exitus.* "Whenever you do not wish to fight, retreat is ever possible. Nothing easier is granted to you than to die." The expression used, "*si pugnare non vultis, licet fugere,*" with reference to the voluntary death which the wise man is free to choose, may leave us perplexed. But the actual context within the ethics of Stoicism as a whole explains what is meant here.

There can be no doubt that when death is sought because a certain situation appears unbearable, from the point of view of virile ethics, suicide cannot be justified. In those very cases where a humanitarian point of view might admit the right to commit suicide, virile ethics cannot excuse it. Still less does it permit a man to take his own life through motives of affection or passion, because this would imply a passive attitude, and one of impotence with regard to one's own spirit, thus deserving con-demnation. Strictly speaking, from the point of view of Stoicism, suicide even for honor or similar motives (i.e., with reference to social conditions), is not admitted.

The Stoic must distinguish between "that which depends on oneself" and "that which does not depend on oneself," and must follow the principle that that which does not depend on oneself does not pledge one's responsibility, must not affect the mind of the wise man, and must not constitute the measure of one's own value or dignity. As we know, this principle of detachment is in harmony with all that which India has regarded as truly spiritu-al. When we consider this, Seneca's maxim can only indicate the importance to be attributed to the inner liberty of a higher being. It is not a question of retreating because we do not feel strong enough to face certain circumstances or trials. It is rather a case

of the sovereign right, which we should always reserve for ourselves, of accepting or not accepting these trials, and also of plac-
ing a limit to them when we no longer see any meaning in them,
or have sufficiently proved to ourselves our own capacity for
overcoming them. Impassiveness thus remains the presupposi-
tion of that maxim, and the right of "exit" is justified only as one
of the factors which may assure us that the vicissitudes in which
we are involved have our consent; that in them we are truly active, that we are not merely making a virtue of necessity. This
point of view is rational and unimpeachable.

Things would, however, present another aspect if we were to
apply the heteronomous framework common to theistic and religious conceptions to the agonistic and virile conception of life.
Cicero attributes to Pythagoras the following saying: "To quit
the post which has been entrusted to us in life is not permissible
without the orders of the Chief, i.e., of God." That is the same
view as that of Catholic moral theology, which actually reaches
the point of condemning these who seek unnecessary martyr-
dom as guilty of sin.

Nevertheless, this appeal to an almost military form of fealty
comes up against certain objections, because it presupposes a
prior free and conscious devotion to a Chief. But from the point
of view of Western religion we cannot speak of this, because that
religious tradition denies that the soul exists before being associated with the body in this life. We suddenly find ourselves in the
"post" mentioned above, because before being there we had no
existence at all; we are thus there without having willed or accepted it. We cannot then speak of responsibility, or of "military
duty," or of a debt for a life received, but not asked for. Hence
the prohibition on suicide has no inner logic; there is only an appeal to faith, a mere acceptance of the will of God.

In Seneca's conception, the horizon is broader and freer; there
remains the idea of finding ourselves through our place in a conflict. And there remains the general command of holding fast,
but the person is conceived as being free, and it is the person
who has the last word. It is thus on the basis of considerations of
a different and interior nature that he must decide as to his own
responsibility and his actual right to his own life.

Up to this point we have dealt with Western points of view. Let us now see how matters stand in a doctrine such as that of the Hindus and particularly that of the Buddhists, in which the implications of Western theism are absent (i.e., the relations between a created being and a creator) and in which man is left to himself and has only to consider the natural consequences of his acts. We believe that the East has a specific and interesting conception only on such a horizon. But from every other point of view the same problems of Western religion present themselves also in the East.

According to the above-mentioned Oriental conception, the same prohibition against suicide of the more usual type is first of all affirmed. Wherever we reach the point of renouncing life in the name of life itself—that is to say on account of one or other form of the will to live and to enjoy—suicide is condemned. (On this point the Eastern view differs little from the Western.) In such cases the act of committing suicide is not judged as a form of liberation, but rather as an extreme, albeit negative, form of attachment to life, of dependence on life. No transfiguration after death can be expected by one who resorts to such violence on himself. In a different state of being the law of an existence devoid of light, of peace, and of stability will simply reassert itself once more. Thus, the problem will in no wise be solved by the act of suicide. Buddhism comes to the point of regarding even the inclination towards extinction, towards nirvana, as a deviation, when it appears as a desire or yearning. It is a Taoist saying that man attempts to free himself from death, but does not try to free himself from life.

At the same time, however, Buddhism, like Stoicism, admits suicide. But in whom? Once again, in a superior human being, in whom the characteristics of the Stoic wise man are to be found further strengthened: in a man who has realized such an absolute detachment that he has gone virtually beyond living and nonliving. Thus it is said that Mara, the demon of this world but also of the world of Brahma, sought in vain for the soul of the ascetic Channo who had "seized the weapon."

Here, however, other difficulties arise. In the first place, if we have attained detachment, what can lead us to choose a voluntary death? In terms of the actual instances cited in the Oriental lore, the meaning does not seem to be very different from what it is in Stoicism. In certain circumstances, there is no reason to involve oneself beyond a particular point. We may "emerge," almost as if we had had enough of a particular game – or as may happen when we wave off a fly, after having allowed it to crawl over our nose for a certain time.

But up to what point can we be sure of ourselves in such cases? He who has attained that spiritual perfection which renders the act permissible can hardly fail to find, in a certain measure, a super-personal significance in his existence on earth, realizing at the same time that this existence, taken as a whole, is but an episode, a transition, "a voyage during the hours of the night," as the Oriental philosophers tell us. Oriental metaphysics in fact admits a multiplicity of states of being, of which the being of mankind is but a particular and contingent one. Once this is admitted, is not a feeling of impatience, of intolerance, even of boredom, evidence of a human residue of weakness? Is it not evidence of something not yet resolved or placated by the sense of eternity, or at least of the great non-earthly and non-temporal distances? And when things are thus, should we not be held, in the face of our own selves, not to act, not to "seize the weapon"?

We should, moreover, also bear in mind another order of considerations. When I speak of "my life," adding that I am free to dispose of what is "mine" at my own good pleasure, I am acting without adequate reflection. In the texts of Pali Buddhism the relativity of this ill-considered talk about what is "mine" is effectively presented to us. It is said in those texts that just as a sovereign has the power of having whomever he wishes executed, outlawed, or pardoned in his own kingdom, similarly if I could say that this body, this life, is truly "mine" and "myself," the wish that it should be so or not be so, could eventually be carried into effect. But that is not the case.

Moreover, strictly speaking, if life were our own in the absolute sense, it should be possible to bring our earthly existence to an end without even a violent act on our own body, but rather through a purely spiritual act. Once more, however, this proves impossible for almost the whole of mankind – only certain special forms of Yoga, of a Tantric inflection, admit the exceptional possibility of the so-called *iccha-mrityu*, of the death at will. This is tantamount to admitting something like an inner bond, a kind of will bound to a life which I cannot regard as extraneous to myself, but which at the same time I cannot identify with my own true will. We cannot fail to take this situation into account. It corresponds to the problem of our own existence as a certain definite sort of being. And any solution akin to that of the knot cut by the sword of Alexander the Great, is not a true solution. The fact of being, united to the impossibility of not being, gives us the disturbing hint of some sort of enigmatic, primal choice — almost as though we were involved and responsible in some obscure manner.

In this order of ideas, however, we cannot go too far when, following the views either of materialism or of Western religion, we consider the principle of life and of consciousness in physical birth. If we accept this, it is difficult finally to avoid a conception such as that of the *Geworfenheit* of certain Western existentialist philosophers: man as the being who finds himself "thrown" into time (in the East one would say into *samsara*), into a "situation" which involves and binds him to a responsibility, yet on a basis that is impenetrably irrational. This obscurity is certainly not solved by bringing in religious faith; indeed, generally speaking, the merit of faith is said to actually consist in accepting without wishing to understand. In the present instance it is a case of accepting a position which, hypothetically, has no connection of any kind, manifest or concealed, with that which may be attributed to my own will. Among Western existentialists, such as Heidegger or Sartre, this faith is atheistic and disconsolate. They do not even believe that the meaning which we are unable to see in our own lives today, might be grasped in a different state of being, as per the resigned hope of the believing Christian.

If we turn to the East, we encounter a different situation. Oriental traditions as a rule have admitted that we exist prior to earthly life, assuming a relation of cause and effect — and sometimes even of a choice — between the real force existing before physical birth and individual existence. (We know, however, that this doctrine was professed also in the ancient West, for instance by Plato and Plotinus.) In this case, although earthly existence cannot be attributed to the mere external will of the Ego, it represents a development associated with a deeper will, but always at the same time forming part of my own integral being. If, therefore, life here below is not an accident, then it cannot be considered a thing to be arbitrarily accepted or rejected. Nor can it be considered a bare and meaningless existential fact, before which there is only the choice of resignation or of a continuous test of resistance. Similarly problematic is the idea that earthly existence is something with which, before we find ourselves in the human state, we have, so to speak, "compromised" ourselves and are to a certain extent implicated—either, if we wish, as in an adventure, or as in a mission, a test, or election, accepting *en bloc* and beforehand even the tragic, problematic, or squalid aspects that the human condition in general may present. With this idea we may give a fairly satisfactory account of what we have just stated concerning the problem as to what may be regarded only conditionally and partially as "mine" and which nevertheless pledges myself.

Traditional Oriental doctrines open similar horizons. As we have already stated, that superiority, or even simply that detachment from life, which alone might authorize us to cast it aside if we wished to do so, can hardly be dissociated from the sentiment of such horizons. We may confer on suicide the significance of an extreme instance establishing our own sovereignty; this is indeed the point most strikingly brought out by the Western Stoic theory. Nevertheless, in few cases does resort to suicide present a positive and intelligible character. Every one of us knows that sooner or later the end will come, which means that the wisest attitude in the face of every contingency should be that of discovering its inner meaning or significance in a wider complex—a complex which, at bottom, according to the above-mentioned point of view, is centered in ourselves and is associated with a kind of prenatal and transcendent will of our own.

We may find an isolated instance in one who seeks death indirectly, along a line in which death and the achievement of the ultimate significance of our own lives coincide—thereby realizing the plurality of the meanings comprised in the Greek word

telos, which signifies the aim as well as the achievement or perfection, and the end. In Western classical antiquity a similar possibility was grasped and justified even on a non-spiritual and
hedonistic plane. At one time, the Roman Senate justified and
even facilitated the decision of him who, feeling that he had attained the apex of a perfect life, had no wish to descend, to subject himself to decay, wherefore he put an end to his own life
happily and willingly. Independently of this, within the order of
ideas considered by us and comparing Western and Eastern
views, we may in a general way set aside the solution (or non-
solution) associated with an act of violence against our own
physical life, that associated with "testing fate" through the
many aspects of a heroic, intense, or even merely hazardous existence. Again in Seneca we find a strange dictum, which may
have some connection with this point: "The wise man casts himself of his own free will into the open abyss." While we do not
remember his exact words, the great Tibetan ascetic Milarepa
used a similar expression.

There are many ways for a detached spirit to submit to "destiny," but a necessary and indispensable inquiry must be undertaken as to the extent to which some deep impersonal reason
exists for a man's continued survival on this earth. And when
this questioning leads us to situations where the border between
life and death is also the limit of significance and fullness of living—thus in a manner different from that which may occur in a
state of exaltation and of mere rapture—then indeed we shall
have attained the best state of mind for realizing all the conditions hitherto considered.

From the consideration of this last point we see that from the
problem we have discussed, with reference both to Western and
Eastern doctrines, practical conclusions may be drawn—
especially with regard to the phase which the West is now going
through. In another article in this volume, we pointed out that it
is not by mere accident that a philosophy, in itself fairly medio-
cre and muddy such as existentialism, should have recently
achieved so much success in Europe. The fact is that it has ech-
oed states of mind which the circumstances of recent times, and
also those now in course of preparation, have widely fostered.

The sense of Heidegger's *Geworfenheit* (the feeling of being "thrown" into the world), of situations from which we may not extricate ourselves, in which for the individual "there is no excuse" (Sartre), plus the growing insecurity of existence, life "being drawn towards extreme temperatures" or towards regions where anonymity in the negative, collectivist sense appears to menace human existence with the total destruction of all meaning and justification: all this is indeed part of the present-day Western world, and it is possible that it may also portend what is to come in the East. In the face of this state of things, existentialism corresponds to the situation of one who finds himself with his back to the wall, without any possibility of escape, at the particularly unstable point of a final inner resistance, beyond which there is nothing left but a complete breakdown.

Thus, this problem may present a certain real interest for a particular type of Western man of today, and for the Oriental man of tomorrow. One who, having lived through what Nietzsche has called "European nihilism," and who, after having realized the problematic character of the value of life, does not feel himself able to face the path of pure detachment — but having integrated his own spiritual horizon with the views set forth above, attempts in spite of everything to find a solution to the human problem along the path of action.

East & West, vol. 5, no. 2 (July 1954): pp. 94–98

ZEN & THE WEST

Zen may be regarded as the last discovery of Western spiritual circles in sympathy with Oriental wisdom. Interest in Zen began to arise in 1927 when D. T. Suzuki published his *Essays on Zen Buddhism*, following a short note which appeared as far back as 1907 in the *Journal of the Pali Texts Society* and some articles in the *Eastern Buddhist* from 1921 to 1939. Another work, Kwaiten Nukariya's *The Religion of the Samurai* (1913), although important, had attracted little attention. On the other hand, after the Second World War, Suzuki's essays were reprinted, not only in the original English edition, but also in a French translation which was very soon out of print.

In France, even a sort of center for studies and publications inspired by Zen ideas has been created, and its chief exponent is Hubert Benoit. In his two volumes entitled *La doctrine suprême* (1952) and in his recently issued work *Laissez Prise* (1954) Benoit has attempted to illustrate certain Zen conceptions in terms of practical individual psychology, also making good use of his own previous experience as a psychoanalyst.

Interest in Zen has also extended to Germany, Switzerland, and Central Europe through translations of particular works. In this connection we may mention Ohasama Shuei's *Zen, der lebendige Buddhismus in Japan* (1925), and Karlfried Graf von Dürckheim's *Japan und die Kultur der Stille* (1950), wherein Zen is considered from the point of view of its influence on the general Japanese outlook on life. Finally, we should mention the intervention of the well-known Swiss psychoanalyst C. G. Jung, who has written yet another allegedly "clarifying" introduction to Suzuki's book, *An Introduction to Zen Buddhism* (1948).

It may be important to study the reasons for this interest which Zen is arousing in the West, outside the specialized circle of Oriental scholars.

From an exterior point of view, these reasons may be connected with some of the so-called surrealist and existentialist aspects of Zen teaching, especially when they have as their basis

the *koan* and *mondo*. These refer to episodes, answers, and dia-
logues concerning the ancient Masters of Zen, abounding in irrational, paradoxical, and sometimes even grotesque elements,
submitted to the meditations of disciples as a means for testing
their capacity to understand that which surpasses the ordinary
categories of logical and discursive thought. In fact, if we stop at
the outward character of these peculiar documents of Zen, we
are led to think of the style and the intentions of certain para-
artistic compositions, which are not only "surrealistic" but above
all "dadaistic," aiming at something which goes beyond a mere
épater le bourgeois by means of jumbles of words and associations
of ideas devoid of logic and unintelligible to common sense.

But this external analogy already indicates the major difference regarding the point to be arrived at. The difference consists
of the presence of a metaphysical background in one case, in
Zen, and in the utter lack of such a background in the second
case, wherein everything is reduced to a disordered urge to eva-
sion, to the will to evoke "the primordial, incoherent, howling,
mad, and burning chaos" (as expressed by Tristan Tzara, the
creator of Dadaism), without any positive element as serving as
a counterpart to a problematic destruction and disintegration of
normal mentality.

Something of the same kind should be said with regard to external affinities between Zen and certain varieties of Western
existentialism. It is often claimed by masters of Zen that spiritual
enlightenment, *satori* or *sambodhi*, intervenes when all the re-
sources of one's own being are exhausted and one is on the
verge of collapse, when, on the intellectual plane, in the fervent
efforts of the disciple, these extreme limits of understanding are
reached, before which the mind both of the common mortal and
of the professional philosopher draws back.

Moreover, proper to Zen is the search for a directly lived and
personal experience, with a strong polemical element against
traditional ethical forms, against conformist rules, writings, and
prescriptions. The Zen ideal of spiritual freedom in certain cases
leads even to iconoclasm and lawlessness. "If you encounter
Buddha or one of the Patriarchs of Zen on your path, kill him,"
says Rinzai, one of the greatest teachers of Zen.

No idol, no image, no outward reference must take us out of ourselves. "Let go your hold" is another word of command, and its meaning is that we should abandon all support, detach ourselves from all ties, both external and internal. To a disciple who thought that he had given proof of emancipation by burning the books of Confucius, the Master said: "You would do better to burn the books which are within yourself."

If to all this we add the fact that the problem of going beyond the conflict between the finite and the infinite—between these two existential elements of individual experience which are co-existing yet contradictory—is a fundamental theme of Zen, it would seem that there is a clear convergence with themes deemed important by existentialism, beginning with Søren Kierkegaard.

But here we must repeat the aforementioned reservation, which now concerns particularly the antecedents of existentialism as "the philosophy of crisis": Western materialism and nihilism, the inherent crisis of all established values. By contrast, Zen has always had as its antecedent, as its background, and as its solid basis, the great spiritual tradition of Buddhism, integrated with certain aspects of Taoism.

It is sufficiently well-known that Zen, in its spirit, may be regarded as a return to the Buddhism of the origins. Buddhism was born as a vigorous reaction against the speculations and empty ritualism into which the ancient priestly caste of India had fallen. Buddha wiped the slate clean, raising instead the practical problem of overcoming that which the popular mind regards as "the sorrow of existence," but which in the inner teaching appears more generally as the state of restlessness, of agitation, of craving, and of forgetfulness of common humanity. Having followed the path of Awakening, of Immortality, himself and without the help of others, the Buddha showed it to those who also felt called.

In the subsequent developments of Buddhism, the same situation against which the Buddha had reacted was to arise again: Buddhism became a religion with its own dogmas, its own ritual, its own scholasticism, its own minute moral rules. Zen once more wiped the slate clean, and raised to preeminence that which had constituted the vital nucleus of Buddhism in its original form: the conquest of enlightenment, of inner awakening. This, in fact, is *satori*.

It is the same *nirvana* that the Mahayana school had already liberated from the outer features of a negative and evanescent reality, and had conceived in the positive terms of *bodhi*, that is to say of enlightenment itself. The Zen doctrine of *satori* brings forward the radical discontinuity between enlightenment and the whole content of ordinary consciousness, but likewise between the actual experience of *satori* and all the methods, techniques, and forms of discipline that may be brought into operation to propitiate it.

If these are the antecedents of Zen, it is clear that nothing of the kind is present in the Occidental mind. The antecedent of Western existentialism is at best the Christian religion, which is quite different from everything Buddhist, because in genuine Buddhism there can be no question of devotional religion in the true sense, and still less of a theistic religion. We have said "at best," because in the more extreme forms of Western existentialism all reference to religion is lacking, and its antecedent is rather the purely nihilistic experience — the "European nihilism" of Nietzsche — which, in the West, has been the logical consequence of a civilization exclusively centered in man and devoid of any transcendent reference.

This leads us to consider a further problem with all the analogies whereby Westerners come to take an interest in Zen. Zen takes over from Mahayana the paradoxical equation *nirvana = samsara*, which is tantamount to the theory of the identity of the immanent and transcendent reality. That which is strictly proper to *satori*, to enlightenment, is an experience in which every antithesis is overcome, in which the finite is perceived in its genuine finitude — wherein all antitheses break down, such as those of spirit and body, "inner" and "outer," subject and object, good and evil, substance and accident, even life and death. A higher unity is the key feature of the being and of the form of experience of one who has secured, as in a lightning flash, as in a sudden ontological alteration of level, *satori*.

It is unnecessary to point out how seductive these horizons

may seem to certain Western minds. No less seductive is the Zen theory according to which we must follow our own nature alone, that all evil and unhappiness come to man from that which is built up artificially by intellect and will, neutralizing and inhibiting the original spontaneity of one's own being. Suzuki does not realize the misunderstanding that he creates when, perhaps with a view to making himself better understood by his Western readers, he speaks in this connection of "Life," and nearly brings Zen into the frame of an irrationalist "philosophy of life."

Now, as a matter of fact, that which in Zen is "Life" and spontaneity of life is actually synonymous with Tao: something very different from the confused notions of an essentially sub-rational and sub-intellectual order, which stand in the center of the immanent and vitalistic philosophies of the West—at bottom merely the decadent by-products of the speculative tradition of Europe.

And here we should emphasize an especially important point: the conquest of *satori* is preceded by a kind of ordeal by fire (a "baptism by fire" as Suzuki says). We must first be capable of absolute self-sacrifice and self-overcoming, of "vomiting completely our own Ego," as a teacher of Zen has said; only after this can the kingdom of a higher spontaneity open up, a spontaneity which we might define as transcendental, referring essentially to the Taoist notion of "acting without acting" (*wei-wu-wei* in Chinese, *musa* in Japanese).

As a counterpart we also have the Zen notion of "acting without merit," of acting without troubling ourselves about sanctions or rewards or finalities associated with all that is particular. This is the very idea of *nishkama-karma*, which, as we know, is at the heart of the Bhagavad-Gita.

In relation to all this, it should also be borne in mind that the Zen ideal is not actually a withdrawal from the world; the true life according to Zen is, on the contrary, life in the world, and no form of activity is excluded. Zen is known for Halls of Meditation (*zendo* in Japanese, *ch'an t'ang* in Chinese), which are a kind of monastic retreat, the discipline of which is by no means less strict than that of many contemplative and ascetic Western or-

ders. Only after having acquired the necessary qualifications in a
zendo (for which many years may be necessary, without any certainty that success will always be achieved), the follower of Zen
returns to the world, if he wishes, and lives the life of the world.
He now lives it having at his disposal the new spiritual dimension which he owes to *satori*.

This makes very clear the difference between Zen and that
Western cult of instinct and spontaneity, which has its roots in a
substratum which we may well call sub-personal. He who
thinks that he can find in Zen the confirmation of a form of ethics of alleged "freedom," but which is instead only intolerance of
all inner discipline, of all command emanating from the higher
parts of one's own being, will be greatly deceived. The spontaneous character of Zen, the freedom which can even go "beyond
good and evil" presupposes an actual "second birth," an event
of which Western immanent and vitalistic theories have not
even a suspicion. We greatly fear that this very misunderstanding is one of the principal reasons for the influence which Zen
can exercise on certain Western minds. In a secondary way another element, likewise a source of misunderstanding, is the polemical attitude which Zen at times takes toward techniques of
Yoga and to the *dhyana* of the type practiced in certain Buddhist
circles.

This would seem to render things even easier: no special discipline would be needed to attain "Awakening." We can here
recognize a legitimate protest against those false interpretations
of Yoga, which present it as a collection of practices and a training which, automatically and without any existential implica-
tion, can lead to extraordinary spiritual results. And yet even
here we fall into misunderstandings.

The fact is that in Zen texts data are rarely given about the entire inner work that precedes the intervention of *satori*, and
about the possibly exceptional predispositions on which it is
conditional. The coming of *satori* is compared to the sudden
ringing of a bell; but an enormous concentration of forces, a
whole development of spiritual tensions precedes that event and
is a condition for it, even if it does not actually bring it about.
Thus, things are not made easier but rather more difficult than

they are where precise techniques and disciplines are indicated. Instead, one trusts the action of the Masters or the accidental circumstances of life which give the final shock whereby the inward eye is opened, which add the last drop whereby the vessel overflows and the "alteration of level" occurs.

We say again that among these imponderables, which make up the antecedents of Awakening, we must include the element associated with spiritual atmosphere and Tradition: they are implications that we do not find in the West, where if *satori* of the Zen type is not excluded, yet for these reasons it constitutes an even more exceptional, unforeseen, and informal event than is the case in the East. A Zen saying is that "Tao may be transmitted only to him who already has it." It may be justly compared with the following dictum of the alchemical Hermetism of the Middle Ages: "If you wish to make gold, you must already have it."

Furthermore, we should consider relations between Zen and Western psychoanalysis. In this connection we are not referring to Benoit, who has limited himself to making use of certain aspects of the method, while with regard to general foundations he has sought to follow the point of view of the teachers of Zen. It is rather the case of Jung who, as we have already said, has written an introduction to one of Suzuki's books, and also elsewhere— for instance, in his commentary on the Taoist text *The Secret of the Golden Flower*, translated by Wilhelm—has attempted to put forth an interpretation of his own.

Jung states that "the analogy of *satori* with Western experience is confined to those few Christian mystics whose sayings for the sake of paradox skirt the border of heterodoxy or have actually overstepped it." In a general way, he holds that in the West Zen would be understood only with great difficulty. In any case, Jung says, "the only movement within our culture which partly has and partly should have some understanding of these aspirations, is psychoanalysis," in the sense of *his* psychoanalysis, which is based on the theory of the vital Unconscious, of the archetypes and of the so-called "process of individuation" (*Individuationsprozess*).

In this there is a misunderstanding even greater than those

we have previously pointed out. To realize this, it is enough to say that according to Jung, the true and positive meaning, not only of religions but also of mysticism and of the initiatory doctrines, would be that of curing the soul torn and tortured by complexes; in other words, it would be to transform a neuropathic and abnormal man into a normal man. In the above-quoted comment he states outright that should symbols and myths, such as those of the Taoists, have a metaphysical and not merely a psychological significance, they would be absolutely incomprehensible to him.

Now what we find in every spiritual and traditional doctrine is something very different. The sound and normal man is here not the point of arrival, but the point of departure, and means are provided whereby he who wishes, if he has the true vocation, may attempt the adventure of effectively overcoming the human condition: or, from a sound man is made a sick one, sick with the sickness of the infinite.

Leaving this aside, Jung seriously believes that the anti-intellectual polemic that is proper to Zen has something to do with the one in which psychoanalysis indulges in the name of Life and of the Unconscious, and that the inner unification and spontaneity produced by *satori* are those secured by the conscious Ego, when, obeying the psychotherapeutic ethics of psychoanalysis, it relinquishes its claim to intellectual superiority and comes to an agreement with the ancestral and even biological Unconscious.

All this is nonsense, if only due to the fact that the Unconscious, conceived as an entity of its own, is unknown to Zen, and that the ideal of Zen is not to integrate oneself into this superstitiously hypostasized Unconscious of psychoanalysis, but to destroy it by bringing light into the subterranean zone of one's own being by means of Enlightenment and Awakening. And again, it is not here a question of "psychological" depths, but of metaphysical and ontological depths, wherein, as we have seen, Jung has openly admitted himself incompetent.

The balance-sheet of our criticism thus seems to be somewhat negative, if Zen is to be considered in its absolute aspect as a doctrine of initiates, like that secret knowledge which, according to Tradition, has been transmitted outside of all written works by Buddha to his disciple Mahakasyapa. But we should further consider Zen according to that which may be derived from it in terms of a vision of life in general and of a particular type of conduct.

In this connection, we must take into account what various authors have brought to light concerning the part which Zen has played above all in Japanese life. Here we also find some doctrines of a general bearing, such as that of an inner calm and of a special meditation, of a brief immobility of the body, and various others which, it appears, are not followed in Japan only by men having an exceptional vocation, but are widespread everywhere.

Somebody has called Zen the religion of the Samurai, that is to say, of the Japanese warrior nobility. In this connection Zen tends to bring about an inner stability, enabling us to act with detachment; in certain circumstances there emerges from it a capacity for self-sacrifice and for heroism which has nothing romantic in it, but is a natural possibility in a being who "has let go his grasp," who has loosened the tie of the Ego. In a general way, this condition of inner steadfastness has been felicitously compared to the hinge of a door which stays firm even when the door is struck.

In a more general way, two other aspects of Zen may be treated. One is the symbolization of even ordinary forms of activity. As a particular instance, it has been said that *Zen-do*, or the way of Zen, is identical with *Ken-do*, or the way of the sword. This means that with an exercise, such as that of the sword, a symbolic significance may be associated, capable of making one foresee the truth of Zen.

To cite another example, the relation existing between the Masters of Zen and the "Masters of tea" has been pointed out; even in a circumstance so commonplace for a Westerner as that of serving and taking tea, the significance of a perfect rite may be concealed.

This brings us to the second aspect of life according to Zen, an aspect which might be summed up in the maxim of Lao-tzu: "To be a whole within the fragment." It is the manner of being wholly oneself in that which one does and in conferring on what one does, whatever it may be, a character of perfection, of completeness. In these circumstances, in every act the whole may be contained, and in every act there may be *satori*.

All these are undoubtedly elements of a superior style of life, elements of a "culture" in the higher sense, of which even the Westerner may appreciate the value, especially in their sharp contrast with all that which in the Western world is agitation, haste, exteriority, disorderly action, and "productivity," without any deep roots. Perhaps it is above all in this connection that the interest of a Westerner in Zen may be devoid of misunderstandings.

But apart from a purely intellectual interest, the measure in which we may also pass to a formative and living action depends on that in which those elements of style may have an autonomy, that is to say, may be detached from a background which, as we have seen, is profoundly different in the East and in the West.

East & West, vol. 6, no. 2 (July 1955): pp. 115–19

AUROBINDO'S
SECRET OF THE VEDA

From 1944 to 1946 the periodical *Arya*—issued in Pondicherry in a limited number of copies and impossible to find anywhere today—published a series of essays by Sri Aurobindo on the secret of the Vedas. These essays have been republished in book form with the same title, *Le secret du Veda* (Paris: Cahiers du Sud, 1954).[1]

These essays are an attempt to shed light on the inner content of the Vedas, starting from the idea that they contain myths susceptible of spiritual interpretation. It is evident that Aurobindo's principal aim is to contest the materialistic interpretation prevailing among many Oriental scholars at the time he wrote. According to a well-known formula, the Vedas deal above all with the superstitious projection of a divine character on the phenomena and forces of nature, with the prayers of the Indian conquerors in order to secure power, wealth, and prosperity, as well as with mythologized reflections of the struggles of the Aryans against the native peoples of the territories into which they had penetrated.

Against this formula, which is now no longer so widely accepted, Aurobindo had an easy task. Every myth and, we may say, every traditional structure of origins, is by its very nature many-sided, so much so that it always also admits, potentially or in actual fact, of a spiritual interpretation. Aurobindo's intention is to contest the existence of a veritable gulf between the "naturalistic" Vedic phase of the Hindu tradition and its subsequent philosophical and metaphysical phase, which took definite shape above all in the Upanishads. His interpretation, from many points of view acute and felicitously presented, of certain typical episodes and of some of the Vedic hymns, show

---

[1] Aurobindo Ghose, *On the Veda* (Pondicherry: Sri Aurobindo Ashram, 1956). Later reprinted under the title *The Secret of the Veda*.—Eds.

us how that secret doctrine of spiritual enlightenment and of the higher nature of the Ego, which was to constitute the central doctrine of the Upanishads, was already contained in the Vedas under mythical garb.

Nevertheless our impression is that, in part, Aurobindo has fallen from one excess into another. While the naturalistic school only saw the outer and coarser aspects of the Vedas, Aurobindo insists perhaps too much on their inner aspect, as though the rest were but a contingent form, thus ending on a plane that is too unilaterally spiritual. In our opinion, when the traditions regarding origins are examined, including the Vedas, we should adopt a more comprehensive point of view; that is to say, we should consider that the cosmic and the spiritual side are closely connected, inasmuch as, according to the felicitous formula of Mircea Eliade, for man at the time of origins "nature was never natural," and in the actual material representations and vicissitudes a superior and inner meaning was secured, sometimes more instinctively as a foreboding, sometimes more consciously held, especially by an elite. But this should not lead us to ignore the "cosmic" aspect through a purely "psychological" interpretation.

Another point in which we cannot altogether follow Aurobindo is his tendency to attenuate the antithesis between the spiritual heritage of the Aryans and that of the aboriginal civilizations of pre-Aryan India.

On the other hand, Aurobindo's fifth chapter is very important, because it gives us the key for a new line of research. It sketches out some systematic principles in the field of philology. Here too it is a question of many meanings. There are original verbal expressions, with reference above all to the roots of words, indicating, so to speak, a "trend" or an "elementary structure," which, according to circumstances, is susceptible of being translated into meanings belonging to very different planes, material and spiritual. This gives rise, by adaptation and specification, to expressions which, objectively, on account of these differences of plane, may appear to have no connection, but in fact are associated by intimate analogies.

An instance given by Aurobindo is *aswa*, the usual meaning

of which is "horse" but that is also used as a symbol of *prana*, the life force. Its root may also suggest, among other things, the notions of impulse, power, possession, and enjoyment. These different ideas are associated in the figure of the charger, in order to describe the characteristic features or *prana*.

From a systematic and epistemological point of view, the importance of recognizing this state of affairs is obvious. Aurobindo ascertained it in connection with the analysis of certain Vedic expressions; but an extension of this principle, if worked out by qualified scholars, cannot fail to open up new and interesting horizons for the science of religion in general.

East & West, vol. 6, no. 2 (July 1955): p. 167

YOGA, IMMORTALITY, & FREEDOM

Yoga may well be said to be that portion of the heritage of Indian wisdom—indeed, of the wisdom of the East as a whole—that is most familiar to Western Europeans and to Americans. Even readers of newspapers and popular fiction of the Somerset Maugham type, have an idea—confused though it may be—of Yoga and the Yogis. Ever since the beginning of the century they have attracted the attention of the West. And here it should be noted that at first, rather than the serious studies made by Oriental scholars, it has been a question of superficial works written less with a view to making the theory known, than for acquainting the reader with the techniques followed to secure results on the spiritual plane and to produce supernormal phenomena. It is known that foremost among these popularizers is Ramacharaka, the pseudonym used by an American. His works, however, have often been mere profanations and distortions. The real substance and final aims of Yoga are often set aside in favor of commonplace applications and adaptations such as physical training, psychic training, the secret of success, deep breathing as a branch of hygiene, mental treatment of disease, Americanized Yoga, and so forth.

Perhaps still more regrettable has been the insertion of Yoga in a vaguely spiritualized framework or in a purely fanciful one. In this field the record has been set by Yogananda's *Autobiography of a Yogi*,[1] a book on the level of fairytales for children which in the West has scored a bestselling success and has been translated into several languages. As Yogananda is a Hindu, it should be noted that the spate of Western popularizers and adapters has been followed by another group of writers exported from India, attracted abroad by the environment pre-

---

[1] Paramahansa Yogananda, *Autobiography of a Yogi* (New York: The Philosophical Library, 1946).

pared by the Western popularizers. This second group has given rise to a dangerous misunderstanding. Persons lacking knowledge and discrimination have thought that the mere fact of being a Hindu sufficed to make a man an authority on Hindu doctrines. Now, for intrinsic reasons due to the essentially esoteric nature of real Yoga, there are good grounds to presume that those Orientals who feel the need to popularize such doctrines and who become, so to speak, commercial travelers, peddling their goods in the West, can only be spurious exponents of their traditions. The same may be said of some Indians who have made themselves readily "accessible" as "masters" in their own country, opening study centers, sometimes provided with typists, an administrative department, a correspondence bureau, etc. As a result of this, it often happens that those Westerners who have succeeded in penetrating and illustrating the real essence of the traditional wisdom of India are asked if they have not been engaged in the construction of some abstract ideal of their own, so different is the level of the teachings they impart from that of the Indians of our day who have become the exporters and vulgarizers of the ancient wisdom.

It is only recently that scientific studies on Yoga by Westerners are keeping pace with those works of divulgation, as contributions in the domain of Orientalism and the history of religions. But here we meet with the obstacle created by the "objective method" which aims at an exclusively exterior, documentary, and informative exactness. It is like undertaking the study of the geometry of solids with the means provided by plane geometry only. In the case of Yoga, if the "depth dimension" be set aside, little remains but an empty husk, of little use not only in the practical but also in the theoretical field; it is little more than an object of curiosity. Nevertheless, in several Western circles which are serious and not merely interested in vague "spirituality," the possible importance of Yoga in its bearing on the problems besetting the modern mind is beginning to be felt. Significant in this connection is the subtitle given to a collection of studies on Yoga recently published by J. Masui: "The Science of the Whole Man."

Another work on the scientific plane recently published is Mircea Eliade's *Yoga: Immortality and Freedom*[2] of which we wish to speak here. Having studied for three years in the University of Calcutta under Surendranath Dasgupta, the well-known author of several books on Indian philosophy and religion, and having spent some time in the ashram of Rishikesh near the Himalayas, Eliade would seem to be in an exceptionally favorable position for dealing with this subject. Nevertheless, we are inclined to think that Eliade's qualifications for the task he has undertaken are not due to these circumstances, except as regards his mastery of philology, his knowledge of the texts, and his general information. In spite of his undoubted talents, Prof. Dasgupta is a markedly westernized Indian who follows the method of "neutral exposition," and the ashram of Rishikesh, like others more or less accessible, is not so much a center of rigorous initiation and supervised practice as an environment whose atmosphere is similar to that of the "religious retreats" of the West. Eliade owes his special qualifications to another source; they derive from the fact that before going to India he had acquired knowledge of metaphysical and esoteric doctrines which as such are not of an "official" character. It is essentially to those doctrines that Eliade is indebted for some points of view that place his works on a different plane from those of most writers on Oriental ideas and the history of religions. All this, however, is not placed in the foreground. Eliade is very anxious to keep in line with the academic world of the West. Among the many hundreds of authors he quotes it would be difficult to find works that do not enjoy definite academic recognition. One might ask if this does not conceal an attempt to introduce a Trojan Horse into the citadel of official culture, an effort which would seem on the one hand to have met with success, as shown by the favorable and unusually prompt reception given to Eliade's works by those circles, but which is not exempt from the danger of "counter shocks."

Our fundamental opinion of Eliade's work on Yoga may be

---

[2] Mircea Eliade, *Yoga: Immortality and Freedom*, trans. Willard R. Trask (New York: Pantheon, 1958).

expressed by saying that it is the most complete of all those that have been written on this subject in the domain of the history of religions and of Orientalism. One cannot mention another that for wealth of information, for comparisons, for philological accuracy, for the examination and utilization of all previous contributions, stands on the same level. But once this has been admitted, some reservations have to be expressed. In the first place it would seem that the material he handles has often got the better of the writer. I mean to say that in Eliade's anxiety to make use of all — really all — that is known on the several varieties of Yoga and on what is directly or indirectly connected therewith, he has neglected the need of discriminating and selecting so as to give importance only to those parts of Yoga that are standard and typical, avoiding the danger that the reader lose track of the essential features by confusing them with the mass of information on secondary matters, variations, and side products. Looking at it from this standpoint, we are even led to wonder whether Eliade's previous book, *Yoga, essai sur les origines de la mystique indienne* (Paris, 1936), is not in some respects superior to this last one, which is a reconstruction of the former. In the first book the essential points of reference were more clearly outlined, they were less smothered by the mass of information brought together, and the references to lesser known forms of Yoga, such as the Tantric and others, were more clearly pointed out.

In the new edition, the scrupulous desire to omit nothing has led to the admission of matter which cannot but give a feeling of contamination. Such are the passages on the relations between Yoga and Shamanism and forms of sorcery, necromancy, and even cannibalism present in the religious practices and in the folklore and magic of the natives. Such relationships, even though so studied as to establish the requisite distances and show the possible "degradations of an ideology due to the incomprehension of the symbolism it contained" may be of interest to the specialist, but they cannot but trouble those who are interested in the superior and "eternal" content of Yoga. Those readers would have preferred that all such references had been either omitted or abbreviated to the indispensable

minimum. Matters of this kind have, moreover, been already
dealt with by Eliade in another of his works, *Shamanism: Archaic Techniques of Ecstasy*, and the present references are often
nothing but lengthy repetitions. They could have been avoided,
thus assuring the new book a character of greater "purity."

But for all this, the reader can clearly see here the supreme
purpose of the true Yoga, which is the attainment of immortality, the "deconditioning" of the human being, absolute freedom,
the active attainment of the "unconditioned." Students of these
subjects know well that in Yoga, as in Indian metaphysics in
general and still more clearly in Buddhism, immortality has a
quite special meaning. In a certain sense, every man is immortal, for according to the doctrine under consideration, death
does not end him, but his life is reproduced in an indefinite series of rebirths. The purpose of Yoga is to destroy this immortality, replacing it by that pertaining to a state free from all
conditionality, whether cosmic or divine.

Eliade calls attention to the fact that existence in the heavens,
divine life, what in Western religions is conceived of as Paradise,
would seem to be a temptation and a trap: one must place oneself at a point beyond all this. In this connection he might perhaps have quoted the *sutra* of the "Invitation of a Brahma" of the
Majjhima Nikaya, where this idea finds its grandest expression.
Attention is also called to the part "cognition" plays in the
achievement of Yoga, which confers on this achievement a character that might be described as "Olympian." The meaning of
cognition as understood by Yoga is indeed that of a "simple
awakening producing nothing, which gives immediate revelation of reality," that is to say, of the true nature of the ego, and
which thus sets us free (p. 42). It is therefore the opposite of a
"conquest" understood in the Faustian and active sense, and this
needs to be realized by many modern Western sympathizers
with Yoga who are following a wrong path.

The opposition between the Yogic experience and the mystic
experience is clearly shown by Eliade. Although he uses the
word "mystic" (see also the subtitle of his previous book) in
speaking of several matters connected with Yoga, this point is
clearly noted by the use he makes of an original expression

"enstasy" instead of ecstasy (see pp. 89 ff). "Yoga is not a technique of ecstasy; on the contrary, it endeavors to realize complete concentration, to attain enstasy." As the meaning of "ecstasy" is "out-standing" so the meaning of "enstasy" is "instanding," a return to the metaphysical center of one's own being as though resuming possession of a throne that has been deserted through that mysterious transcendental fact that Hindu tradition designates by the expression *maya*. While Eliade stresses this opposition particularly in the case of Shamanism, it also holds good morphologically for the relations between Yoga and mysticism.

Thus Eliade interprets as "enstasy" *samadhi* itself, the ultimate aim of classical Yoga. And he thus also overcomes the errors of those who, knowing nothing of experiences of this kind, believe that this ultimate term is a kind of trance, a condition of reduced consciousness, almost of unconsciousness ("a zero point between consciousness and unconsciousness" as Rhys Davids said, referring to *nirvana*), whereas it is really a state of super-consciousness. The strange thing is that not only Westerners have fallen into so gross an error. We have, for instance, seen D. T. Suzuki suggest an interpretation of this kind (even if in defense of Zen as a specific tendency), in relation to the Yoga of Samkhya and similar Mahayana doctrines.

It would perhaps have been useful to develop in this field a comparison between the horizons of Yoga and those of psychoanalysis. All those Westerners who believe they have made such an extraordinary discovery with their psychoanalysis (Jung goes as far as to assert, presumptuously, that psychoanalysis alone makes "scientific understanding" of Eastern wisdom possible) should realize that the positive side of psychoanalysis had been discovered many centuries ago, by Yoga as part of a complete knowledge of man, and not by that mutilated, deformed, and contaminated anthropology which provides the basis of Freudianism and of all its more or less orthodox derivatives.

However, reservations must be expressed as regards that which arouses the vocation for Yoga. From the external, historical point of view it is true that Yoga arose from the need of a practical (and, we would add, active) experience of sacred things and as a reaction against metaphysical speculations and fossilized ritual. But when it comes to the existentialist motive, we are far from agreeing with Eliade when he writes: "Freedom from suffering, that is *the* principal aim of all Hindu philosophies and all Hindu mysticism" (p. 26). It may appear to be so if only the more popular exoteric aspects of the teaching are taken into account. But this is not true even of Buddhism, as we have shown in one of our works (*The Doctrine of Awakening* [London, 1951], pp. 59 ff.); after Shcherbatskoy had already shown (*The Central Conception of Buddhism* [London, 1906]) that a deeper meaning could be given to *duhka* than the vulgar one of "pain." The very word *klicta*, applied to states of consciousness suppressed by the practice of Yoga, properly means "impure" (in a metaphysical, not in a moral sense) and does not mean "painful." The real starting point of Yoga (and of Buddhism itself) is the reaction of a soul aspiring to the absolute against a contingent, unstable existence, conditioned by agitation, subject to change—existence that includes in its affective aspects both pain and pleasure and even the beatitude of the most radiant celestial gods. What Eliade states is therefore incorrect, although the book contains enough material to lead us to a correct view of things.

In the early chapters of the book, Eliade uses a "vegetative" analogy to describe the Yogic mode of existence, which also seems to us unsuitable. Recourse to a "mineral" analogy would be better suited. It would better express Yogic immobility, the "arrest of the flow," the concentration of consciousness on "being" as opposed to "life," and its ritual expressions also: the immobility of the *asana*, the impassiveness of the features, etc.

It would perhaps be better, when dealing with the state of existence that must be overcome, not to introduce the notion of "history," an exclusively Western notion. In the world of Hindu metaphysics, the basic idea is, instead, that of *samsara*, of purely irrational becoming. This differs markedly from the notion of "history" and even from the simple condition of temporality for, in the Hindu conception, *samsara* and the world of *maya* are inclusive of states in which time, as we know it, is non-existent. We have made this observation because Eliade has a special personal notion of his own, which, though it supplies a valuable and legitimate key for the interpretation of many things in the world of myths and rites, is not applicable to all cases. We are dealing here with the motive of the destruction of "history" by the return to the prehistoric and atemporal state of the origins. This scheme can be applied wherever cyclical structures are in evidence. We do not think there is much place for it in the field of Yoga, however. Eliade himself has said what is really at issue: a "break of the level," not only of the level of human, historical experience, whether individual or collective, but also of the cosmic level. The legitimate point of reference is, therefore, that of a doctrine of the multiple states of being, seen as a *vertical system*, whereas the idea of a pre-temporal (prehistoric) origin implies always a residuum of "horizontalism." At a certain point in *samsara* there is an arrest, after which one proceeds not so much backwards as upwards, liberating oneself from all conditioning circumstances. This is a metaphysical itinerary, which in the ancient Western civilization was expressed by the symbolism of the journey through successive planetary spheres and the progressive "unclothing" that took place in each of them, while an equivalent of this is given in the Tantric Yoga by the ascent of consciousness transported by the power of the *kundalini* through the seven *chakras*.

We have referred to Tantrism, and one of the principal merits of Eliade's book is that it has dealt fully with this current of Indian spirituality, still little known in the West and which, when it has been studied at all, has been generally decried because of its connection with sex magic and the use of women. While remaining faithful to the style of "neutral" exposition, more especially in this matter, Eliade suggests the key to interpretations of undoubted value, based always on extensive documentary evidence, as when dealing with the rites of "transubstantiation," "polyvalent languages," etc. So also on the matter of "hyperphysical physiology" or "subtle physiology," which plays an important part in Tantric Yoga, Eliade sets himself apart from the materializing opinions formulated by some Orientalists and some physicians who are ignorant of the very principles underlying such notions.

But as Tantric Yoga follows a course which differs widely from that followed by classical Yoga, it would seem likely that important results might have been obtained by engaging in research along typological and morphological lines. It seems to us that in several cases the different forms of Yoga arise not only from technical differences but from a difference in the spirit that inspires them. The background of Tantric practices, which is to some extent immanentist, differs substantially from the transcendent one of the Yoga of the strict type and of the Patanjali school. Jñana Yoga and Hatha Yoga (taking the latter in its deeper sense which is not that of "physical Yoga") may have definite, distinct implications in their general vision of the world (we have referred to it in our work *The Yoga of Power*[3]). We may set up the ideal of liberation against the more positive one of liberty—and here we may refer to the Tantric Siddha and the Kaula whose antinomianism has precedents in some strains of the most ancient Upanishads and Brahmanic literature. The stress laid on the importance of the body in its esoteric aspect may also afford a clue, while it is quite clear that the process of conferring cosmic meaning on the body may have a significance of its own which must be referred back to the spirituality of the Vedic origins, and contrasts with the ascetic trends of a dualistic background.

These considerations lead us to the much-debated problem of the origins of Yoga. It would seem that Eliade is inclined to believe in a non-Indo-European, non-"Aryan" origin. In his first book, this view was stressed more and was extended to cover not only Yoga but part of Hindu ascetic tendencies in general. As is well known, some inquirers with racial views had already formulated the theory that all forms of asceticism and practices of mortification of the flesh were foreign— *artfremd*—to the spirituality of the Aryan conquerors of India, and that all such notions in Hinduism should be traced back to exogenous influences and to a world outlook no less foreign.

---

[3] Julius Evola, *The Yoga of Power*.

At first the reference made here was to Dravidian and Kosalian natives; later on the question arose of the archaic civilization brought to light by the excavations at Mohenjo-Daro. It is claimed that among the objects found at Mohenjo-Daro there are figures in the postures—*asanas*—of Yogis and ascetics, along with divinities who are not found in the Vedas, but who play an important part in many currents of Yogic, ascetic, and also devotional intonation of the later period. All this strikes us as rather problematic, for we believe that in such matters morphological considerations must be decisive. Eliade writes: "In so far as Yoga represents a reaction against ritualism and scholastic speculation, it adheres to the aboriginal tradition and stands against the Indo-European [i.e. Aryan] religious heritage" (p. 361). He adds, "[T]he absence of the Yoga complex from other Indo-European groups confirms the supposition that this technique is a creation of the Asian continent'" (ibid.). This is not quite right. As regards the first point, we may note that early Buddhism was also a reaction to ritualism and speculation, but it was of purely Aryan origin, starting with the person of its founder. For the rest, the consideration of historical metaphysics must be introduced in a morphological framework that we have already outlined elsewhere (in the already quoted *The Doctrine of Awakening* and also in our *Revolt Against the Modern World*[4]). Account must be taken of that regression of mankind from the spirituality of the origins, to which the traditions of all peoples bear witness and to which, indeed, Eliade himself makes frequent reference in the course of his researches. As a result of this regression, states of spirituality which in the beginning had an almost natural character and were at the basis of a sacramental and ritual conception of the world, were later on attained only exceptionally as the result of ascetic and violent practices. In our opinion this is the historical place of Yoga also, as *spirit*. In other Indo-European traditions it is matched by the Mysteries and initiation practices which, though varying widely in form and method, have the like significance of an experimental *opus restaurationis* and occupy the

---

[4] Julius Evola, *Revolt Against the Modern World*.

same position of Yoga when considered in relation to the origins. It may be that in the framework of Hindu spirituality, the transition to a phase of this kind, which corresponds to Yoga, was favored by exogenous influences: *favored*, not *determined*. Beyond possible exterior resemblances of themes, we must consider the possibility that, when passing from one civilization to another, they acquired a markedly different meaning. Thus, for instance, it seems pretty certain that the Mohenjo-Daro civilization was essentially a "Mother civilization," a civilization of the "Divine Woman" with a tellurian or lunar background belonging morphologically to the same cycle of southern, paleo-Mediterranean, and even South American civilizations. The classic spirit of Yoga is, on the other hand, exclusively virile and uranic. We have knowledge of an asceticism which was known also to the Mother civilizations (from the Maya to the Babylonians). But it had a character of mortification which is quite absent from Yoga. Even the central theme of that civilization, the Divine Woman, is revived in Hinduism, through the Tantric metaphysics, in a strongly spiritualized form which would be unaccountable if it were not related to the Aryan heritage and to the Upanishads themselves, while its original features survive only in the reemergence of popular orgiastic or devotional cults.

The examination of these problems would lead us far afield. But in any case it seems to us that Yoga should be considered only as an integral part of Indo-European spirituality of the purest kind. For this reason, also it seems to us that the search for relations with the drosses of Shamanism as they are present in the origins of the Aryan peoples, or elsewhere, is of no interest. The only thing of interest, as we have said, is the definition of the autonomous features of a spiritual phenomenon which should be examined where it arose in conformity with its "idea" and therefore in its typical imperfection, liberating itself from empirical conditioning factors.

After this glance at the contents of Eliade's new book we are tempted to ask him a somewhat prejudicial question: to whom is the book addressed? As we have openly declared, it is a fundamental work for specialists in the field not only of Oriental research, but also of the history of religions. In his introduction, however, Eliade states that the book is addressed also to a wider public and he speaks of the importance that a knowledge of a doctrine such as that of Yoga may have for the solution of the existential problems of the modern Westerner, confirmed as that doctrine is by immemorial experience.

Here complications arise. To meet such a purpose, it would be necessary to follow a different plan and to treat the matter in a different way. A Westerner who reads Eliade's book may be able to acquire an idea of Yoga as "*la science intégrale de l'homme* [the integral science of man]," he may acquire knowledge of a teaching that has faced in practice as well as in theory the problem of "deconditioning" man; he will thus add yet another panorama to the many provided him by modern culture. His interest will perhaps be more lively than the "neutral" interest of the specialist; he may flirt with the aspects of a "*spiritualité vivante*." But on the existential plane the situation will be pretty much the same as it was before, even if the information available is deeper, more accurate, better documented. The possibility of exercising a more direct influence could only be sought from a book addressed to those who have shown an interest in Yoga and similar sciences not because they seek information but because they are seeking a path; a book that in this special field would remove the misunderstandings, the popular notions, the deviations, and the delusions spread by a certain kind of literature to which we referred at the beginning of this article; a book displaying the accuracy and knowledge that we find in this work of Eliade, in so far as it is an exposition kept within the limits of the history of religions. Such a book has perhaps still to be written. But even so the essential need would not be met, for it is the unanimous opinion of the true masters of Yoga that the key to their science cannot be handed on by the written word.

East & West, vol. 6, no. 3 (1955): pp. 224–30

ANCIENT ORIENTAL &
MEDITERRANEAN EROTIC
SYMBOLISM

The theme of an original duality or polarity related to that of the sexes occurs in the traditions of almost all cultures. This duality is sometimes expressed in purely metaphysical terms, sometimes in that of divine or mythological figures, cosmic elements, principles, gods, and goddesses.

It seemed evident to earlier modern historians of religion that this was due to anthropomorphism. In their opinion, as man had created his gods in his own image, so also he had transferred to them the sexual differentiation proper to the mortal beings of this earth; and therefore all those dualities and divine dichotomies were simply the product of imagination and human sexual experience was their only real content.

The truth is just the opposite. Traditional man endeavored to discover in divinity itself the secret and essence of sex. For him, the sexes, prior to their physical existence, were present as super-personal forces, as transcendent principles; before appearing in nature they existed for him in the sphere of the sacred, of the cosmic, of the spiritual. It was in the multifarious variety of divine figures, differentiated as gods and goddesses, that he tried to seize the essence of the eternal masculine and of the eternal feminine, of which the opposite sexualization of mankind is but a reflex and one particular manifestation.

Therefore the views of the historians of religion to which we have referred must be inverted. Instead of human sex affording the basis from which to see what there is of truth and reality in the sexually differentiated mythological and divine figures, the key to an understanding of the deeper and more universal aspects of sex in man and woman is to be found precisely in these figures.

But in addition to this we have many examples of doctrines which, starting from the two principles, the male and the female, have explained the process and the various stages of the world made manifest—taking, moreover, those two principles as the basis for a special morphological understanding of the inner side of the phenomena of the nature, spirit, and life of man, both as an individual and as a species.

The most notable example of such teaching is afforded perhaps by the Chinese doctrine of the *yang* and the *yin*. *Yang* and *yin* correspond indeed to the cosmic male and female; they are the two fundamental determinations or categories (*erh-hsi*) of reality, as well as the two chief forces which, in their various combinations and forms of equilibrium, define the nature and specific form of all that exists within and outside man. Thus we find already in the I Ching, the fundamental text of the whole Chinese tradition, the possible combinations of the signs of *yang* and *yin* variously grouped in trigrams and hexagrams, presented as the keys to an understanding of all the processes and transformations of the world made manifest.

The doctrine of Hindu metaphysical Tantrism concerning Shiva and Shakti or other equivalent deities, is much the same. They express the metaphysical duality of pure motionless being and of power-substance or power-life. Uniting with power-life as with his spouse (Shakti has the double meaning of power and of spouse) the God gives rise to manifestation. Just as in the Far-Eastern conception of *yang* and *yin* as omnipresent and determining, so likewise in the Hindu conception powers and conditions going back to Shiva and Shakti, to the cosmic male and female, are everywhere active in reality. Thus a text makes the goddess say: "As in the universe everything is at the same time Shiva and Shakti, so Thou O Mahesvara [the male god] art everywhere and I am everywhere. Thou art in everything and I am in everything."[1]

We find likewise in the ancient Western world several equivalent conceptions: the duality of matter and form (Aristotle and Plato), of *nous* and *psyche*, of *ousa* the eternal being and *ousia* the substance power of the eternal masculine, which bring

---

[1] In J. Woodroffe, *Creation as Explained in the Tantra* (Calcutta, s.d.), p. 9.

us back to the same order of ideas.[2] To this conception we are
equally brought back by all sexually differentiated figures of
mythology and of the cults of the ancient world.

In the following considerations we would like to fix our attention on a special application of these ideas, touching, on the
one hand, the philosophy of civilization, and on the other the
ideals of spiritual realization. For this purpose, we shall start
from a specific theme of sexual symbolism. On the first point we
owe to Bachofen[3] the most important contribution to a "sexology
of civilization": an attempt to group systematically the various
forms of worship, ethics, outlook on life, conception of the beyond, of law, of social institutions on the basis of the special relation ascribed to the two principles of the primordial dyad, the
cosmic male and female, by the several cultures or several stages
of the same culture.

The great morphological antithesis with which we are thus
confronted is that between the uranian and the tellurian cultures, between the culture of the Mother or of the Great Goddess
(Magna Mater Deorum) and the culture of the Father, or of the
male Olympian God. As a social reflex of these two fundamental
conceptions, characterized by the preeminence of the female
(demetric or aphroditic) principle or of the male principle, we
have the gynaecocratic or the androcratic type of society; a duality of which, however, the matriarchal or the patriarchal societies
are only the extreme cases, for a civilization may develop under
the female symbol without being necessarily a matriarchy.

The fecundity of the leading ideas set forth by Bachofen as
early as the last century, and applied by him essentially to the
study of the ancient Mediterranean world, has not been adequately grasped, though several other later scholars have come
to similar conclusions in their more specialized researches, often
without perceiving it. It has not even been noted that starting
from the same premises valuable clues can be found for compar-

---

[2] See for instance Plotinus, *Enneads*, III, vii, 4; III, vii, 10; III, viii, 1;
I, i, 8; III, ii, 2; V, viii, 12.

[3] J. J. Bachofen, *Das Mutterrecht* (Basel: 1870); *Myth, Religion, and
Mother Right*, trans. Ralph Manheim (Princeton, N.J.: Bollingen, 1967).

ative research in fields that Bachofen had hardly taken into consideration, e.g., in the study of different forms of spiritual, mystical, or initiatic experiences. In fact, it is well known to the student of the science of religion that in this field also sexual symbolism has played a large and important part. In a way, even Christian mysticism has adopted the symbolism of marriage, speaking of the "bridegroom" and of the "bride," and of a spiritual wedding. This last idea is but a sublimated reflex of the motif of the *hieros gamos*, so widely spread both in the ancient world and in the Orient.

Now, it may come as a surprise what wealth of significance we can associate in this field with a special form of symbolism which to the uninitiated may seem rather shocking, the symbolism of the inverted embrace. This symbolism can be studied within the frame of two traditions, the paleo-Mediterranean and the Hindu.

On the one hand we have the Egyptian goddess Nut. This ancient Egyptian goddess is one of those representations of the cosmic feminine who, like Isis herself, seems originally to have had a telluric significance, i.e., an essential relation with the Earth, but who in the course of time acquired a celestial character and a supremacy in a gynaecocratic conception of the universe. Identified by Plutarch with Rhea, the Great Goddess of the Mediterranean area, Nut appears at a given moment as the "great Lady who gave birth to the gods," the "Lady of Heaven, the Sovereign of the two Earths," who wields the papyrus scepter and holds the key of life. In one of the most frequent representations, Nut is "she who bends": "almost always nude, she arches her body until she touches the earth with her finger tips, while her legs and arms seem the pilasters supporting her horizontally placed body." Nut in this posture is the sky, and she is not alone: stretched on the ground beneath her is Geb, conceived as the god of the earth (thus with inverted meanings, for the sky had always been referred to the male, the earth to the female element) with the male organ erect, and the whole image leaves no doubt that Nut is about to lower herself and lie on the supine god to join with him and take him into her flesh in the sacred union, the sacred *mixis* of Heaven and Earth. Pestalozza, to whom we owe the above description, rightly notes that the unusual inverted position of the goddess in the embrace adumbrates a definite symbolic ritual meaning. This position is met with not only in the Egyptian representations but recurs also in the Sumerian and Elamite world, and in the bas-relief of Laussel it takes us back to the Paleolithic age. The principle of female sovereignty finds in it a curiously drastic expression. The superimposed position of the goddess signifies ritually the prevalence of the female element in a gynaecocratically directed culture, her supremacy affirmed and asserted in the very exercise of the act through which life is perpetuated.[4]

But there is also a spiritual counterpart of this situation. It is to be found in the ancient Mediterranean Mysteries in which the source of the sacrum was recognized in the Divine Woman, the Great Goddess — Demeter, Cybele, Mylitta, Ishtar, etc. — and the participation in it was linked with orgiastic forms that led to ecstatic, devirilizing states. It was thus that at the climax of frenzy in the rites celebrated in the mysteries of some of these goddesses — especially of Cybele — the devotee went so far as to emasculate himself, a brutal and insane act, in which one can nevertheless see the material symbol of a form of ecstasy implying dissolution of the male principle, the very opposite of a supernatural integration of the ego, the personality. This "spiritual feminization" is confirmed by some details of the ritual, such as the female apparel worn by the initiates and priests of some of these cults, and also by the fact that often these goddesses had only priestesses assigned to their worship. In some cases "sacred prostitution" was practiced. By copulating in a sacrament with the priestesses or with the consecrated virgins (the so-called *parthenoi hieroi*) in whose shape the goddess was invoked, one expected to obtain participation with the sacrum.

If we move to the East we find the archaic continuity of these forms of gynaecocracies, for the substratum of pre-Aryan India

---

[4] See on all this Uberto Pestalozza, *Religione mediterranea* (Milan: Bocca, 1951), Chapter II and pp. 71 et seq.; cfr. p. 51 where it is mentioned that in some texts of the Pyramids this position is assigned to Isis herself.

and its ramifications show the importance given to the central motif of a female divinity, a great Goddess, often worshipped, in India also, with orgiastic rites. But just as in the ancient Mediterranean world, where the gynaecocracies with their cults and mysteries found themselves confronted by the spirituality of the purely Hellenic stock descended from the North, directed toward androcracies and Olympian divinities, so again in India we witness a decided shift in outlook, which occurred even in the schools that most felt the influence of the pre-Aryan legacy, such as Hindu and Indo-Tibetan Tantrism. A significant indication of this may be found precisely in the motif of the inverted embrace, of which we find traces also in the cultures directed towards androcracy, but with a totally opposite meaning. In passing, it may be mentioned that this type of embrace was condemned by the Islamic peoples in a definite symbolic context, because it is said: "Cursed be he who makes of woman the sky and of man the earth."[5] But in Hindu and Indo-Tibetan iconography the representation of the divine couple in *viparita-maithuna* are well known and very frequent. This is the name given to an embrace characterized by the immobility of the man and the movement of the woman, therefore repeating substantially the Egyptian representations of Nut and Geb. Here, however, the same symbol is used to express the opposite idea of male sovereignty.

The reference is essentially to the doctrine of the Sankhya on the metaphysical dyad *purusha-prakriti*. *Purusha* is the spiritual male principle, "inactive," immobile; like the "unmoved mover" of Aristotle, who is pure being which, by a kind of catalytic action, causes motion by its mere presence: the becoming in "nature," *prakriti*, conceived as the cosmic feminine principle and the material cause of creation. The Tantric and other schools have taken up these views again; hence the symbolism of Shiva and of other deities of the *"purushic"* type, represented as joined in an embrace with his Shakti (his "bride" or demiurgic force), in which the active role is played by the woman. The idea expressed by this erotic symbolism is that real virility does not act in a material way; it only awakens movement, commands it

---

[5] H. Bartel, *Experiences chez les Arabes* (Tunis, 1904), p. 302.

(whence also the Tibetan symbol of Vajradhara, the "Scepter-bearer," who in this iconography often takes the place of Shiva), gathers the fruit as the enjoyer. Movement in itself as pure dynamism, as "desire," as "energy" directed outward without having in itself its own principle, belongs instead to the feminine principle, cosmologically to nature, *prakriti* or Shakti, the material cause of the manifestation, its "mother": not to Shiva, the motionless Scepter-bearer. We thus have a complete inversion of meanings, not only in relation to the conceptions of gynaecocracy, but also, and perhaps even more, to those of modern activism and of the Western "religions of life." The latter, directed towards a philosophy of becoming rather than of being, seem in spite of all appearances, really to have lost the sense of what virility is in its superior manifestations.

The following remark should also be made: if we run through the leading Hindu treatises on profane eroticism, such as the Kamasutra and the Anangaranga, it would not seem that the *viparita-maithuna* is a position much in use in the current love manifestations of those countries. It would seem, therefore, to belong essentially to a symbolic and ritualistic plane, and to have the value of *mudra* or *asana* in order to express the meaning referred to above. But this holds good in more than just iconography.

As is well known, sexual magic and sexual Yoga appear in Tantrism. They are a part of the so-called secret ritual, of the Hindu *pancatattva*, of Vajrayana or Buddhist Tantrism and of the Sahajiya schools. Here, by means of a special regime of the embrace, the actual sexual experience with a young woman, consecrated and carefully trained, paradoxically becomes one of the techniques for obtaining existential rupture: liberation, participation in the Unconditioned. Now, one of the names by which this practice is known is *lata-sadhana*; *lata* is the name given to the woman used in these rites, in which she acts as an incarnation of the Devi, of Shakti, Durga, or Tara. The literal meaning of *lata* is liane, climbing plant, which refers to one of the postures of the *viparita-maithuna* (here equivalent to *latavestitaka* and *vrikshadhirudhaka*). We thus see that even in the real initiatic use of the woman, the special ritual posture gives the tone to a particular spiritual trend that may be considered in net opposition to the ecstatic participations in the sacrum as they are conducted by the gynaecocratic Mysteries. This claim is corroborated by other facts. In the sexual *sadhana* of the Vajrayana we find among the meanings that the human couple is to incarnate ritually those of *upaya* for the man, and of *vidya, prajna,* or *bodhi* for the woman[6]; those are two principles on which a cosmological as well as a Yogic interpretation is conferred by that doctrine; it is from their union that perfect liberation springs. Now, the anti-ecstatic active nature of this achievement is clearly shown by the fact that a passive, feminine character is attributed to the enlightening and transfiguring force, to the knowledge or wisdom — *vidya, prajna* — it is like the woman in the nuptial embrace in which the role of the male is instead played by the "operating power," *upaya*.

There is still another point to consider. The Mahayanic doctrine of the *trikaya,* of the three "bodies" of the Buddha, is well known. Now the doctrine of the Vajrayana teaches that the non-dual state, the supreme achievement that can be attained by means of sexual practices and which is associated with *sahajasukha* or *paramahasukha* can lead still further; there is indeed talk of a "fourth body," *sukha-kaya,* in which the ecstatic state or *nirvana* — if conceived as a transcendence detached from the world — is surpassed. In that "body," the Buddha, joined in a "sublime embrace" — *alingara* — with the Shakti, possesses perfect enlightenment — *sambodhi* — also the root or primordial power of all manifestation.[7] This might be described as a super-ascetic realization which leads beyond the dualism of *samsara* and *nirvana,* the exact opposite of all pantheistic dissolution, of all naturalistic ecstasy under the sign of the Demeter-like and telluric Magna Mater.

One last hint may be offered by the ethics of the Vira, Kaula, and Siddha, that is to say of the Hindu Tantric schools of the

---

[6] Cf. S. Dasgupta, *Obscure Religious Cults* (Calcutta: University of Calcutta, 1946), pp. xxxvii–xxxviii.

[7] Cf. L. De la Valle Poussin, *Bouddhisme,,* p. 134; H. Von Glasenapp, *Buddhistische Mysterien* (Stuttgart: Spemann, 1940), p. 161.

"Left-Hand Path" — *vamacara* — which employ the "secret ritual," with *maithuna*. We have here an ethic of the "superman," that would make Nietzsche turn pale. He who travels along this path is *dvandvatita*: superior to all opposites (good and evil, shame and honor, merit and demerit, etc.), not only as a detached being but also as *svecchacari*, as a man for whom his own will is the only law, for whom all the laws, rules, and rites of the ordinary "bound" man, *pasu*, have fallen away. This may, of course, lead to dangerous deviations. The path — as the texts state — may be compared to walking on a razor's edge or to riding a tiger.[8] However, as for the corresponding spiritual atmosphere, there can be no doubt about an absolutely "virile" attitude, an attitude all the more important as we are here dealing at the same time with schools in which the Shakti, in its various epiphanies and cratophanies, plays an essential part.

Even this brief excursion into the world of paleo-Mediterranean and Oriental traditions shows what interesting horizons lie beyond the veil of the metaphysics of sex; it shows that erotic symbolism was capable of fixing essential meanings and differentiations affecting the highest peaks of spiritual elevation and the border lines between contrasting visions of the material and the sacred world.

East & West, vol. 7, no. 2 (July 1956): pp. 156–61

---

[8] On all this see J. Woodroffe, *Shakti and Shakta* (Madras: Ganesh, 1929), passim and pp. 580 et seq.

ZEN & EVERYDAY LIFE

Eugen Herrigel
Zen in the Art of Archery
New York: Vintage, 1999
[*Zen nell'arte del tirar d'arco* (Turin: Rigois, 1956)]

Kakuzo Okakura
The Book of Tea
Berkeley, Cal.: Stone Bridge Press, 2006
[*Il Libro del Te* (Rome: Fratelli Bocca, 1955)]

The first of these little books, translated into Italian from German, is unique of its kind, as a direct and universally accessible introduction to the spirit, the fundamental disciplines, and the behavior of the civilization of the Far East, especially Japan. Herrigel is a German professor who was invited to teach philosophy in a Japanese University, and decided to study the traditional spirit of the country in its most typical living forms. He took a special interest in acquiring an understanding of Zen Buddhism, and, strange as it may seem, he was told that the best way to do so was to study the traditional practice of archery. Herrigel therefore untiringly studied that art for no less than five years, and the book describes how his progress therein and his gradual penetration into the essence of Zen proceeded side by side with archery, conditioning one another reciprocally, leading to a deep inner transformation of the author himself.

The essence of Zen as a conception of the world is, as is well known, its special interpretation of the state of nirvana which, partly through the influence of Taoism, is understood in Japan not as a state of evanescent ascetic beatitude, but as something indwelling, an inner liberation, a state free from the fevers, the ordeals, the bonds of the ego, a state which may be preserved while engaged in all the activities and in all the forms of everyday life itself. Thanks to it, life as a whole acquires a different dimension; it is understood and lived in a different way. How-

ever, the "absence of the ego" upon which Zen insists so strongly, is not akin to apathy or atony; it gives rise to a higher form of
spontaneous action, of assurance, of freedom and serenity in action. This may be likened to the situation of a man who holds on
compulsively to something and who, when he lets it go, acquires
a higher serenity, a superior sense of freedom and assurance.

After calling attention to all these points, the author notes the
existence in the Far East of traditional arts that both arise from
this freedom of Zen, and offer the means for attaining it through
the training required to practice them. Strange as it may seem,
the Zen spirit dwells in the Far Eastern arts taught by the Masters of painting, serving tea, arranging flowers, archery, wrestling, fencing, and so forth. All these arts have a ritual aspect.
There are, moreover, ineffable aspects thanks to which true mastery in any of these arts cannot be attained unless one has acquired inner enlightenment and transformation of ordinary self-
consciousness, which makes mastery a kind of tangible sacrament.

Thus, Herrigel tells us how in learning to draw the long bow,
little by little, through the problems involved in this art as it is
still taught in Japan, he came to the knowledge and the inner
understanding that he sought. He realized that archery was not
a sport but rather a kind of ritual action and initiation. To acquire a thorough knowledge of it one had to arrive at the elimi-
nation of one's ego, overcome all tension, and achieve a superior
spontaneity. Only then, paradoxically, was muscular relaxation
joined to maximum strength; the archer, the bow, and the target
became one whole. The arrow flew as if of its own accord and
found its target almost without being aimed. Stated in these
terms, the mastery attained is a degree of spirituality, or "Zen,"
not as theory and philosophy but as actual experience, as a
deeper mode of being.

By describing situations of this kind, based on personal experience, Herrigel's little book is important not only because it introduces the reader to the spirit of an exotic civilization, but also
because it enables us to view in a new light some of our own ancient traditions. We know that in antiquity, and to some extent
in the Middle Ages also, jealously guarded traditions, elements

of religion, rites, and even mysteries were associated with the various arts. There were "goods" for each of these arts and rites of admission to practice them. The initiation to crafts and professions in certain guilds and *"collegia"* proceeded along lines parallel with spiritual initiation. Thus, to mention a later case, the symbolism proper to the mason's art of the medieval builders served as the basis for the first Freemasonry, which drew from it the allegories for the proceedings of the "Great Work." It may therefore be that in all this the West once knew something of what has been preserved to this day in the Far East in such teachings as "the way of the bow" or "the art of the sword," held to be identical with the "way of Zen" in a singularly positive form of Buddhism.

The author of the second little book, to the Italian edition of which we now turn, is a Japanese interested above all in aesthetic problems, who has studied the modern schools of art in Europe and America but has remained faithful to his own traditions and has resolutely opposed the introduction of Europeanizing tendencies in his own country. The central part of his *The Book of Tea* confirms what we have just been saying.

There have been close connections in the Far East between Zen, the "tea schools" and the "tea ceremony" (the term used by the author to designate this is "teaism,"[1] an infelicitous word given that "theism" indicates in our countries every religion based on the notion of a personal God). Indeed, it is claimed that the tea ceremony as elaborated in Japan in the 16th century was derived from the much more ancient Zen rite of drinking tea from one single cup before the statue of Bodhidharma. Generally speaking, this ceremonial rite is one of the many forms in which the Taoist principle of "completeness in the fragment" is expressed. Lu-wu in his book *Cha-ching* had already asserted that in preparing tea one must observe the same order and the same harmony that from the Taoist standpoint governs all things.

The author adds that it is part of the religion of the art of life. "The tea became a pretext for the enjoyment of moments of meditation and happy detachment in which the host and his guests

---

[1] Not in the English edition. — Eds.

took part." Both the site and structure of the rooms built for this special purpose—the tea-rooms (*sukiya*)—follow the ritualistic principle; they are symbolic. The variegated and partly irregular path that, within the framework of the Ear Eastern art of gardening, leads to the tea-room is emblematic of that preliminary state of meditation that leads to breaking all ties to the outer world, to detachment from the worries and interests of ordinary life.

The style of the room itself is of refined simplicity. In spite of the bare and poverty-stricken appearance it may offer to Western eyes, it follows in every detail a precise intention. The selection and the use of the right materials call for great care and attention to detail, so much so that the cost of a perfect tea-room may be greater than a whole casement. The term "*sukiya*"—the author says—originally meant "the house of imagination," the allusion being not to wandering fancies but to the faculty of detaching oneself from the mundane world, of recollecting oneself and taking refuge in an ideal world.

Other expressions used by the Masters of the tea ceremony are "the house of emptiness" and "the house of asymmetry." The first of these expressions traces back directly to the notion of the Void proper to Taoist metaphysics (and here we may recall also the part played by this notion, almost as a key or background in the "aerial" element of Far Eastern painting). The expression "house of asymmetry" refers to the fact that some detail is always intentionally left unfinished and care is taken to arrange things to give the impression of a lacuna. The reason for this is that the sense of completeness and harmony must not arise from something already fixed and repeatable, but must be suggested by an exterior incompleteness which impels one to conceive them *inwardly* by means of a mental act.

The author also deals with the connections existing between the art of tea and that of selecting and arranging the flowers in the *sukiya*, here again in conformity with symbolism and a special sensibility. Often one single flower rightly selected and placed is the only ornament of the "house of emptiness."

Lastly the author reminds us that a special philosophy of daily life is accessory to the tea ritual, so much so that in current Japanese parlance a man lacking in sensibility to the tragicomical sides of personal life is said to be "lacking in tea," while those who give way to uncontrolled impulses and feelings are said to have "too much tea." This brings one back to that ideal of balanced, subtle, and calm superiority, which plays so large a part in the general attitude of the man of the Far East.

If we think of the wide use made of tea in the West, and of the circumstances of this use in our social life, more especially in fashionable circles, it would be natural to draw comparisons which would show that, even in this seemingly commonplace field, as on the plane of ideas, all things of the Orient are diminished when imported into the Western world.

East & West, vol. 7, no. 3 (October 1956): pp. 274–76

SPIRITUAL VIRILITY
IN BUDDHISM

It is the fate of almost all religions to become, so to say, *dena-tured*: as they spread and develop, they gradually recede from their original spirit, and their more popular and spurious ele-ments, their less severe and essential features, those furthest removed from the metaphysical plane come to the fore. While hardly any of the major historical religions have escaped this fate, it would seem that it is particularly true of Buddhism. We need only consider the prevalent notion of the teaching of the prince of the Sakyas that has been formed not only in the West by those who profess admiration for Buddhism, but also for many centuries past in many strata of the peoples of the East.

The terms in which the 2500th anniversary of the death of the Buddha has been commemorated this year, and the way the message that the Buddhist religion should have for the modern world has been spoken of, afford evidence of this.

Someone has recently been able to say: "There is no other al-ternative: the world today must choose between the H-bomb and the message of the Buddha" — thus identifying that mes-sage with pacifism and humanitarianism. The Western friends of Buddhism have been almost unanimous in appraising it as a sentimental doctrine of love and universal compassion, a doc-trine composed of democracy and tolerance, to be admired also for its freedom from dogma, rites, sacraments; almost a sort of secular religion.

It is true that these distortions appeared quite early in the history of Buddhism. But though it may seem audacious on our part, we have no hesitation in saying that this is a *falsification* of the message of the Buddha, a degenerated version suited not to virile men, standing with head erect, but to men lying prostrate in search of escape and spiritual alleviation, for whom the law and discipline of a positive religion are too severe.

If we accept the interpretations referred to, Buddhism in its real essence would be a system of ethics rather than a religion in the strict meaning of the term. This character, which some historians of religion had stressed in an attempt to charge Buddhism with supposed inferiority as compared to theistic and dogmatic religions, is today claimed by others as a merit, their claim being based on a misapprehension of a different, but not less serious kind. If Buddhism, taken in its original forms, cannot be called a "religion," this depends on the fact that it is not *below* but *above* the plane of all that can be legitimately defined as "religion," especially theistic religion. The doctrine of awakening and enlightenment, the essential core of Buddhism, has nothing "religious" about it, because it is preeminently of an "initiatic" or esoteric character, and as such is accessible only to a few elect. It therefore represents not a "broad way" open to all (as in more than one of its aspects, almost in its very name, *Mahayana*) but a "straight and narrow path" reserved for a minority. This is already made clear by the accounts given in the Canon of the first moment of the enlightenment of the Buddha. When Prince Siddhartha had the revelation of the truth and of the way, the *dhamma*, he resolved not to spread it, believing it to be inaccessible to the masses, to ignoble natures immersed in *samsara*. And so, from the way the story is told, it would seem that only through the mythical intercession of certain divinities the Buddha was induced to change his mind and to consent at last to communicate the possibility of the Great Liberation and the path to attain it.

It is known that in the beginning the Order of the *Arya*, the noble "sons of the son of the Sakyas," was restricted, even if not by extrinsic limits. Thus for instance, the Buddha objected to the admission of women. And those who like to see in the attitude of the Buddha towards the conception of caste and the exclusiveness of the Brahmanas, evidence of an egalitarian and universalist spirit, are much mistaken. They confuse that which lies beneath the differences and limits proper to every sound hierarchy (as is the case with democratic egalitarianism, whether social or spiritual) with that which lies above such differentiated structures, as in the case of the truly awakened Buddhist and of the initiate in general. The comparison drawn between the Awakened One and a flower that rises miraculously from a heap of dung[1] is very eloquent on this point, even if it be not edifying to those who indulge in a democratic and humanitarian interpretation of Buddhism. Considered in the framework of the Hindu situation of his day, the Buddha was a revolutionary only in so much as he opposed to the fictitious and obsolete dignities—corresponding no longer to real qualifications—true dignity, to be shown in each case by works and effective superiority. Thus, for instance, he maintained the designation of Brahmana, but opposed the type of the real Brahmana to that of the false one.[2] If in the case of Buddhism one can speak of universalism, this is the universalism of the summits, not the promiscuous one at the base.

The reduction of Buddhism to mere moral teachings appears as the height of absurdity to anyone who remembers the canonical parable of the raft. In no spiritual tradition more than in Buddhism is the purely instrumental and provisional character of morality, of *sila*, so strongly stressed. As is known, the whole body of moral rules, with good and evil, *dhamma* and *adhamma*, was compared by the Buddha to a raft that is built for crossing a river, but which it would be ridiculous to drag along once the crossing has been made.[3] Contrary to the view, whether philosophical or religious, which ascribes to moral rules an intrinsic, autonomous value (a typical instance of this is the so-called "absolute morality" of Kant's categorical imperative) the Buddha ascribed to his attitudes of right conduct a purely instrumental value, the value of means justified only in view of a certain aim and therefore only *sub conditione*. But this end, as are the higher grades of Buddhist ascesis and contemplation, is beyond morality, nor can it be measured by the religious conception of "holiness." As Milarepa was to say: "In my youth I committed some black deeds, in my maturity some white ones; but now I have re-

---

[1] Dhammapada, 58–59.

[2] Cf. Sutta Nipata, I, vii, 21; Digha Nikaya, XII, 1. 24–26, 28; Dhammapada, 141.

[3] Majjhima Nikaya, XXII.

jected all distinctions of black and white."[4]

Thus, the fact that some of the rules of the *sila* may perhaps correspond to what the moralists desire, should mislead no one. The spirit inspiring the action in the two cases differs fundamentally. This holds good also for that which the "spiritualists" admire so much in Buddhism: the ethics of love, of compassion, of harmlessness. He who follows the path of awakening cultivates these mental attitudes only as the means to free himself from the bonds of ignorance, of the samsaric ego; not out of sentimental altruism. A conception such as the Western one, expressed by the words "God is love," and the consequent absolutization of this sentiment, would be an absurdity for the authentic Buddhist doctrine. Love and compassion are mere details of the *opus remotionis*, whose aim is a liberation, an enlargement or opening of the soul which can favor, in some cases, the "rupture of the level" and the sudden flash of illumination. Thus, not only is the famous series of the four *brahmavihara-bhavana* or *appamanna*, which includes love and compassion, technically and practically equivalent to the several states of a purely "dry" intellectual contemplation, leading to the same goal (the four *jhana* and the *arupa-jhana*), but even in the series of *brahmavihara-bhavana*, the last stage, *upekkha*, is impassibility, the disincarnate neutrality of a soul that has become free from all sentimentality, from both the bonds of the "I" and the "thou" and shines as a pure light in an ontological super-individual essentiality expressed also in the symbol of the "void," *sunna* or *sunnyata*.

We are not the only ones who have noted that this concept of the void is not only affirmed by the Mahayana, but is found already clearly stated in the Canon of early Buddhism. The work proper to Mahayana has been rather that of making this concept the object of a paradoxical philosophical elaboration (paradoxical because this idea corresponds to an absolutely super-rational level detached from philosophy), to which Mahayana added a popular soteriological religion which carried the

---

[4] *Vie de Milarepa*, trans. Kazi Dawa Samdup (Paris: A. Maisonneuve, 1955), p. 81.

misdirected interpretation of the precept of compassion to a form that, *inter alia*, leads to a flagrant contradiction in this form of later Buddhism. In fact, on the one hand, the precept of compassion and love for all beings is announced to such a degree that the Mahayanic *Bodhisattva* vows that he will not enter *nirvana* until all living creatures have been redeemed; while on the other hand, according to the Mahayana doctrine of the universal "void," all these beings are non-existent, so many illusions, mere apparitions of the cosmic dream generated by ignorance. This nonsensical contradiction alone should suggest that to the precept spoken of, and also to the doctrine of universal illusion, a meaning must be given that differs widely from the exoteric, literal, and popular one attributed to them. Both should be understood on a purely pragmatic plane.

In some aspects of the Mahayana, in which alone the esoteric doctrine of the "awakening" has been replaced by a "religion," and also in other currents, the essential core of Buddhism has been enveloped by philosophical, mythological, and ritualistic dross and superstructures. When considered in relation to them, so-called "Zen Buddhism" stands for a return to the origins, a reaction in all respects similar to that of early Buddhism itself to degraded Brahmanism. Now, Zen throws into clear relief the essential value of illumination, its transcendence of all that which, in several cases, may favor it—and at the same time its immanence, that is to say the fact that the state of enlightenment and *nirvana* does not mean a state of evanescent ecstasy, an escape, so to say, of which compassion is only a pale reflex accompanied by horror of all that is action and affirmation. It is instead a higher form of freedom, a higher dimension. For him who holds fast to it there is no action that cannot be performed, and all bonds are loosened. This is the right interpretation of the doctrine of the void, of the non-ego, and also of the Mahayanic conception of the identity of *nirvana* and *samsara* in a third principle higher than either, and anterior to both. This should be recalled to those who accept unilaterally the theory of harmlessness, of the timorous respect of all forms of life. As a matter of fact, Zen Buddhism could be called the doctrine of the Samurai, i.e., of the Japanese nobility[5] who are certainly not noted for their abhorrence of arms and bloodshed. The fact is that all this wisdom turns on one pivot alone: the severance of the bond of the ego, the destruction of ignorance, the awakening. When the bond of the ego is severed, all restrictions cease. The fruit the doctrine will bear depends on the human soil on which its seed falls. The humanitarian, pacifist, vegetarian image of the Buddhist is a distortion, and in any case its acceptance is not compulsory. Samurais and *kamikazes* may equally well be Buddhists. In a book in which a Buddhist chaplain describes the days of the Japanese put to death by the Americans,[6] we see how these men died without conversion or repentance, in a perfect state of Buddhist grace; men who, if they were not "war criminals" as the victors claimed, were as generals, officials, and politicians certainly not delicate, shy flowers of the field.

Those who have experienced that fundamental inner transformation, that "rupture of the level" which is the essential feature of Buddhist realization, are in possession of an unshakeable calm, an "incomparable certainty" which not even the age of the H-bomb and of all the other devilry of the modern world can disturb. This calm can be preserved above all tragedies and all destructions, even when man's human and ephemeral aspect is involved. Now, it is in this direction rather than in any other that we find the message Buddhism may have for our time. At the conclusion of one of our works[7], in which we tried to reconstruct the essence of the Buddhist doctrine, we pointed to the dual possibilities it offers. The first is that of a clear and virile *askesis* which creates in man firmness and serenity, *samatha*, by means of a carefully constructed mental practice which allows the detachment and strengthening of a principle

---

[5] Kaiten Nukariya, *The Religion of the Samurai* (London: Luzac, 1913).

[6] Shinsho Hanayama, *Heiwa no Hakken* (Tokyo: Shibazono Shobō, 1949). Translated into Italian by G. Morichini, in the Bocca edit., under the title *La Via della pace* (Rome: Bocca, 1954); and into English by Hideo Suzuki, Eiichi Noda, and James K. Sasaki, under the title *The Way of Deliverance* (London: Gollancz, 1955).

[7] J. Evola, *The Doctrine of Awakening*.

that transcends the purely human, irrational, emotional, and, in general, *samsaric* substance of our being. In no other tradition are these practices taught in such a clear, thorough, we might say *scientific* form, free from specific religious or ethical implications. What here is of particular importance is the style of the clear vision, *yatha bhutam*, which is that of a superior realism, the vision exactly corresponding with reality. A goodly number of gifted men can still make an "immanent" use of Buddhist teachings thus understood. We may even find in them the corrective of the prevalent trends of our day: the religion of life, of struggle, of "becoming," the union with irrational, instinctive, and sub-personal forces that urge man ever onwards in a "flight towards" (Bernanos), destroying in him all centrality, all real constancy. In an age like ours, *samsaric* as no other has ever been, the Buddhist system of free and virile *askesis* as preparation for ultramundane realization might serve to create limits, to provide inner means of defense, to keep at bay the anguish or the rapture felt by those who cling convulsively to the illusory mortal Ego. To repeat, this is not to be understood as an escape, but as a means for assuring a serene and superior security and liberty. And in view of the times that are approaching, perhaps we have never needed men educated along these lines as much as we do now.

But in the Canons we find juxtaposed to the use of such disciplines for life, the use of them for carrying us "beyond life."[8] It is here that Buddhism presents itself as the doctrine of awakening, identical with a strict doctrine of initiation, which as such is timeless (*akalika*), not tied down to historic contingencies, superior to all faiths and all systems of mere devotion. It is not easy for the Westerner to realize what the real purpose of Buddhism is on this level. The ideal here is absolute unconditional being, the attainment of absolute transcendence. By now the puerile idea of those who identify *nirvana* with "nothingness," or regression into the unconsciousness of a trance caused by the distressing knowledge that "life is suffering," has been to a large extent discarded. Also, the teaching that "life is suf-

---

[8] Cf. for example Majjhima Nikaya, LII.

fering" belongs only to the exoteric aspect of Buddhism. The deeper meaning of the term *dukkha* is "commotion," agitation rather than "suffering": the condition that the *arya*, the "noble son," rejects is that of universal impermanence, of the transitory—a state that should therefore be essentially understood in ontological terms, and whose emotional significance is quite secondary. Its counterpart is thirst, *tanha*; and the extinction, the *nirvana* in question, is not destruction in general but precisely and only the destruction of what in our being is thirst, insatiable longing, fever, and attachment, in all its many forms and ramifications. Beyond all this lies awakening and enlightenment, the *samadhi* which leads to the unconditioned, the immortal.

Perhaps the antithesis between the initiatic notion of "awakening" and the religious and more especially Christian notion of "salvation" or "redemption" has not yet been adequately stressed. The religious conception is based on the assumption that man is a being existentially detached from the sacred and the supernatural. Because of his ontological status as creature, or as the result of original sin, he belongs to the natural order. Only by the intervention of a transcendent power, or on the assumption of man's "conversion," or by his faith and his renunciation of his own will, only by Divine action, can he be "saved" and attain to life in "paradise."

The implications of the concept of "awakening" are entirely different; man is not a fallen or guilty being, nor is he a creature separated by an ontological gulf from a Creator. He is a being who has fallen into a state of sleep, of intoxication, and of "ignorance." His natural status is that of a Buddha. It is for him to acquire consciousness of this by "awakening." In opposition to the ideas of conversion, redemption, and action of grace, the principal theme is the destruction of "ignorance" (*avijja*). Decisive here is a fact of an essentially "noetic" or intellectual, and not emotional, nature. This confers an indisputable aristocratic character on the doctrine of Buddhism. It ignores the "sin" complex, self-abasement, and self-mortification. Its *askesis* is clear and "dry"; it is alien to the features of auto-sadism or masochism which are always present in the forms of the asceticism better known to the West, and which have often given rise among Westerners to anti-ascetic prejudice and a distorted exaltation of life.

This character of loftiness, which is founded in Buddhist ontology, is matched by the Buddhist doctrine of autonomy: man is the free master of his own destiny. He alone is responsible for what he is. Thus, in conformity with his vocation, he can affirm the state he is in, or he can change it. There are no penalties and no rewards; therefore, there is nothing to hope for and nothing to fear. The only thing that must be taken into consideration is the objective, unsentimental, extra-moral connection of cause and effect. If a Buddha sets himself free, it is by his own efforts alone. On the path leading to awakening, no external aid is to be sought. This conception, on which the traditional Hindu notion of *karma* was already founded, is particularly stressed by Buddhism. The historical Buddha, as is well known, did not present himself as a divine savior, but as a man who, after attaining enlightenment and the Great Liberation by himself, indicates the path to those having a like vocation. All this refers to early Buddhism. With Mahayanic Buddhism in its prevailing and popular aspects, we descend once more to the level of the soteriological religions; innumerable Bodhisattvas and Buddhas busy themselves to insure the salvation and happiness of all living beings.

Again, if we turn to the *terminus ad quem*, to the ultimate ideal of Buddhism, the break with religious conceptions is a clear one, and it is difficult for Westerners to fully grasp. In the West we are accustomed to consider paradise as a religious ideal, the survival of the believer in heaven, and only a few mystics speak of the unitive life, of union with Being. But the Buddhist doctrine looks on all this as trivial and leaves it behind. Its horizon is that of the traditional Hindu metaphysics, which considers the divine worlds as themselves belonging to *samsara*, and immortality not as the perpetuation of individuality but as the realization of the Unconditioned. Nor is Being the supreme point, that beyond which nothing other is conceivable. Being is matched by Non-Being, and the Unconditioned is that which is superior and anterior to both. In a well-known passage[9] the Buddha rejects and condemns one by one all the identifications: identification with the body, with the elements, with the Ego, with the cosmos, with the divine hierarchies, even with the God of Being, that is to say with Brahma. In a speech which is Michaelangelesque in its grandeur, identification with the God of Being, which is equivalent to the *unio mystica*, the ultimate limit of religious rapture, is rejected in terms that see it almost as a diabolical temptation,[10] for it would represent a limit to the great Liberation, to the attainment of the Unconditioned.

He who has a knowledge of these dimensions of the Buddhist experience, dimensions that appear clearly in the canonical texts, what can he think of those who consider Buddhism to be not even a religion but a system of sickly sentimental secular morality, consisting of humanitarianism and indiscriminate love, the pale evanescent wisdom of those who have recognized that the "world is suffering"? Undoubtedly, the metaphysical dimensions of Buddhism just discussed can only be understood, let alone reached, by very few. But this is indeed the ultimate background of the whole system. The canonical saying goes: "All the waters of the ocean have but one flavor, that of salt; so the sense of the whole of the Law is only one, that of liberation."[11] For the ultimate, the great *nirvana*, or more correctly, the "void," the *sunna*, the Buddha uses the method of the so-called "negative theology"; it is unnamable, indefinable, incomprehensible to the human mind; one can only say what it is not, not what it is, for one cannot even apply to it the category of Being. But how to ignore what may be called the traces, the marks of Him who has no marks? Because "the lord of men and gods" was called the perfect "awakened One." As "unconquered and intact beings," similar to "lofty Overmen," appear those who have travelled along this path[12]; like lions in whom both anguish and terror

---

[9] Majjhima Nikaya, I.

[10] Majjhima Nikaya, XLIX.

[11] Anguttara Nikaya, VIII, 19.

[12] Majjhima Nikaya, CXVI.

are dead.[13] They see the past, they see the heavens and the infernal regions,[14] They know this world and the world beyond,
the kingdom of death and the kingdom free from death, the
temporal and the eternal.[15] They are "like tigers, like bulls in a
mountain cave" though they appear as "beings free from van-
ity, who have appeared in the world for the good of many, for
the health of many, for compassion of the world, for the good,
the profit, and the health of men and gods."[16] "I have passed
beyond the brambles of opinions, I have acquired power over
myself, I have reached the path, I possess the knowledge, I
have none who guide me," says the Awakened One of Himself.[17] He is the "daring One who never hesitates, the sure
guide, free from passion, bright as the sunlight, free from
pride, heroic"; he is the "One who knows, who is dazzled by
no fevers, overcome by no troubles, tempted by no victories,
stained by no stains"; He is "the great being who lives apart,
freed from all ties, no longer slave to any servitude"; He is the
"worthy One who keeps watch over Himself, of steady step,
ready for the announcement," "inclined to none and disin-
clined towards none, sublime in soul, powerful, impassible";
He is "the One whom no thirst burns, no smoke dims, and no
mist wets; a spirit who honors sacrifice and who rises up ma-
jestically as does no other."[18] Passions, pride, falsehood have
fallen away from Him like mustard seeds from the point of a
needle. Beyond good, beyond evil, he has cast off both chains,
and detached from both pain and pleasure he is purified.
Since He knows, He no longer inquires: "How so?" He has
reached the bottom of the element free from death. He has left
the human bond and the divine bond and has freed Himself
from all bonds; no one in the world can conquer Him, who has
for his domain the infinite and whose path is known neither by

---

[13] Suttanipata, III, vi, 47.
[14] Samyutta Nikaya, III, 58–59; Dhammapada, 422–23.
[15] Majjhima Nikaya, XXXIV.
[16] Ibid., IV.
[17] Uraga Vagga, III, 21.
[18] Majjhima Nikaya, LVI.

the gods nor by angels, nor by ordinary men.[19]

Notwithstanding the hyperbolical element in some of these attributes, an ideal type takes definite shape from them against a background of grandeur and spiritual virility which it would be hard to find in any other tradition, in comparison to which the religious value of "sanctity" is pale and flaccid. Judged by this standard, far from being a doctrine accessible to all, a doctrine that makes things easy for the "spiritualists" because it has no dogma and no rites and is free from exclusivities, the Buddhist path of awakening is a narrow one reserved for those who possess an exceptional vocation and qualifications. In following it, it may be said that the saying of the *Katha Upanishad* is also applicable: it is like walking on a razor's edge without help, either human or divine.

It is agreed that wisdom of this kind cannot be "popularized." Indeed, it should not even be indiscriminately communicated, for it is not without risk. The Canon itself speaks of the consequences of the doctrine if wrongly interpreted: it is like one who, having seized a serpent in the wrong way, sees it pounce on him, causing death or mortal pain. The doctrine stands out and remains a summit, bearing witness to what a superior humanity could conceive. As to the forms in which Buddhism has become a religion *sui generis,* and, worse still, as to those forms in which it is conceived and appreciated as a democratizing humanitarian morality, they should be rightly considered as an unmitigated contamination of the truth.

East & West, vol. 7, no. 7 (January 1957): pp. 319–27

---

[19] Dhammapada, 420 sg. and passim; Majjhima Nikaya, XCVIII.

SOL INVICTUS:
ENCOUNTERS BETWEEN EAST & WEST IN THE ANCIENT WORLD

Franz Altheim's recently published book, *Der unbesiegte Gott: Heidentum und Christentum* (*The Unconquered God: Heathenism and Christianity*; Hamburg: Rohwolts Deutsche Enzyklopädie, 1957), should be of special interest to the readers of this journal, for it deals with a significant encounter between the ancient civilizations of East and West.

Altheim's book is a study of the political and religious conditions in the late period of the Roman Empire, a period which has not yet been thoroughly studied. It is usually slurred over as the time of Roman decadence, but it was really one of the most interesting periods of ancient history, with its violent contrasts of light and shadow. There was something demonic about it; passions and ideas were driven to extremes, exceeding human limits, while every now and again flashes of religious radiance illuminating the most turbid, tragic, and problematic situations.

In his new book, which is lucid, acute, and brimming with information, Altheim explores this world, following the clue offered by sun worship and its fortunes. The starting point is in the East, but this book deals not with the ancient Egyptian and Iranian forms of the solar cult but those of a later period which had its center in Syria (the Land of the Sun according to an ancient conventional etymology), that is to say, with the cult of Helios of Emesus.

Another of the misused formulas that we find in the historiographers of late classic antiquity would have us believe that Rome had been "Asianized," had given up her most genuine traditions, and had gone over to foreign cults, customs, and deities, most particularly Asian and Afro-Asian. That a foreign element had penetrated into Rome certainly cannot be denied; the penetration had indeed begun in the 3rd century BC.

However, one of the main theses that Altheim repeatedly asserts in his work on the history of Roman religion is that we should not seek for the specifically Roman element in the particular and narrow native traditions of the early days, but rather in the specific and original character that Rome stamped on all that she gradually took over, thus conferring on it a higher significance. Often, indeed, the encounter with an exotic element served Rome as an incentive to revivify her own forms.

This is also noted by Altheim in the case of the solar cult. It was no mere nature cult, as was supposed by a history of religions that has now been to a great extent surpassed and which we need not discuss. The ancients did not adore the stars as such, i.e., as physical realities, but as symbols of sacred, spiritual powers. Though mingled with spurious elements, the Sun God, thus understood, had been the object of widespread worship among the peoples of the Eastern Mediterranean, and in the late period of the Empire this cult had gradually penetrated the world of Roman civilization. Septimus Severus had already begun to raise such figures as Serapedes, Heracles, Dionysus (the two latter in their non-classical form) to the rank of gods of the Roman State, identifying them by analogy with traditional Roman deities. After him, Caracalla was the first to style the Sun God as *invictus*. Ten years later this god was to become the chief divinity of the Empire.

The first phase of this penetration was, however, characterized by violent and turbid incidents connected to the Emperor Heliogabalus, whose very name was that of a Syrian solar deity. He tried to introduce the cult into Rome in its more spurious and aberrant Oriental forms, and appointed himself as the high priest of the cult, officiating in ways that could not but give rise to violent reactions among Roman traditionalists. With the downfall of Heliogabalus this first phase came to an end, and would seem to have been nothing but an extravagant interlude.

However, Rome of that age felt more and more keenly the need for strengthening and defending herself on the spiritual, intellectual, and religious plane, just as she had done on the political and military one. This was also connected with the struggle against the advance of Christianity. Hence the *sacrum studium litterarum*, of which Macrobius speaks, understood as a return to the classics to ensure the spiritual renewal of the Empire. This was the path by which, after the first reaction had died down, the solar god was to reappear and become the center of a new kind of theology of the Empire, the spiritual environment being, moreover, prepared by Neoplatonic speculations and by writings that had spread far and wide, such as the *Aithiopica* of Heliodaurus of Emesus.

Thus, we find solar symbols appearing more and more frequently on Roman coins and ensigns. *Deus Sol Invictus* are the words that always recur. The radial crown of the Emperors is a solar symbol. At last, with the Emperor Aurelian, the cult of the Sun God takes its place in Roman public worship, though purified in a way that reveals the original formative power of Roman civilization, of which we have already spoken.

Under this influence, the solar divinity loses those spurious and equivocal Syrian features and is invested with a Roman and Olympian form, that of the deity most characteristic of the pure Roman tradition, Capitoline Jove, *Jupiter optimus maximus*. Unlike his Asian antecedent, this divinity is no longer surrounded by goddesses, no longer copulates, has no offspring, and has less of a relation to the physical symbol of the sun as an entity that rises and sets.

Above all, it is a luminous, spiritual, abstract symbol of power at the center of the universal Empire of Rome, whose leaders it consecrates and invests. The priests of this cult are no longer strangers brought over from Syria (as Heliogabalus attempted) with their unseemly, even orgiastic ceremonies: Roman Senators form its college, which is placed on the same footing as the austere one of the *Pontifices*. Finally, the symbolic birth of the God at the winter solstice, characteristic of all the oriental solar divinities, becomes the official Roman festival of the 25th of December (the *Natalis Solis Invicti*, the Roman precursor of what was to become Christmas). It was decided that every four years, on that day, a great and brilliant gathering was to be held in honor of the Invincible God, the god both of the Empire and of the Imperial Armies.

While Altheim has duly followed all these developments, there are perhaps two points that deserve special attention.

The first is the connection that existed between the solar theology of the Empire and the Mysteries of Mithra. The epithet *Invictus* was also applied to the symbolic figure of Mithra, whose cult spread widely in the Roman Legions. This reference is important as it enables us to penetrate into the deeper, inner meaning of that attribute. *Invictus* is the sun understood as the light which each morning triumphs over darkness. In the realm of the mysteries this was transferred directly on the spiritual plane to the ceremonies through which the initiates participate in the nature of Mithra as expressed by this symbol. Thus the outer cult of the Emperor, and the solar attributes ascribed to him, in principle acquired an inner counterpart which in its higher sense was spiritual, related as it was to the world of the Mysteries and to the experiences proper to that world.

The second point has a more general bearing. In his previous works on the history of the Roman religion Altheim has called attention to the error committed by those who would oversimplify talking of the "Hellenization" of the Roman religion after its Italic origins. He has shown that "Hellenization" in its more important aspects, more particularly those connected with the reception of the great Olympian divinities, was more a revival or reintegration of a very ancient common inheritance which, among the Italic peoples, had often been obscured and debased by the influence of the cults prevailing in the pre-Indo-European Mediterranean world.

In the case of Rome, instead of referring to Hellenization as a mere passive estrangement, one should rather speak of a return to original sources *through* Greece, following a line of continuity, and in many cases of a passage from potentiality to actuality, from germinal and inchoate forms to fully developed ones. Rome received and took to herself Greek divinities because she found in them more perfect expressions of religious intuitions that already formed part of her inheritance, although in more confused, incomplete, and, we might almost say, mute forms. These are Altheim's original views of Hellenization, which seem to us largely correct.

Now, something similar may be noted in the case of the solar cult of late Roman antiquity. We find, moreover, valuable material in support of this assumption already in Altheim's book. The special references to the Sun God of Emesus should not make us forget that, on the one hand, the Syrian cult was only one particular expression—a particular *Erscheinungsform*—of a spiritual orientation that took many other shapes, all of which lead us back—some in metahistorical and morphological, others, however, in historical terms—to one primordial Tradition, from which they originate. This is why, as has been noted and is well known, the ritual date of the winter solstice, as the birth of light or of the new light, belongs to a vast and widely ramified cultural cycle, carrying us back even to Hyperborean prehistory.

It is really just this last point which has been treated by Altheim when dealing with the Illyrian Emperors, and above all with Aurelian. Referring to the Imperial solar cult, he shows that this Emperor selected many symbols formerly pertaining to all the most ancient Nordic traditions: symbols found also in pre-Roman Italy (those found in the Val Camonica are of special importance) and which Altheim in other works has been able to connect with the migratory waves of those who were the distant progenitors of the Latins, i.e., of the future founders of Rome.

Following the threads of these virtual and real convergences, we are led to a truly significant hypothesis. May it not be that the Imperial solar cult, instead of being an imported Asianized phenomenon, represents the revival of a primordial Tradition? And just as it affirmed itself in Rome at that period as a State cult, this worship possessed an Olympian purity and dignity of its own, no longer to be found in the residual local cults scattered over the Near East and elsewhere. No one will fail to grasp the importance that such an interpretation would have for the universal significance of ancient Rome. It is one, moreover, which we have had occasion to suggest, in a wider context, in one of our books.

Another point that Altheim takes into direct consideration is no less interesting. It is the relation of the Romanized solar cult with the earliest forms of Christianity, to which the subtitle of his book refers.

It is a fact that the image of a divine solar sovereign had a decisive influence on Constantine himself, the Christian Emperor.

On this matter Altheim has brought together documentation that is little known. Constantine preserved in large measure the symbols of the previous solar cult. Until 317, the *Sol Invictus* appears on the imperial coins of Constantine, even though we see on them also the image of the Sovereign bearing the labarum with the Cross. The *Sol Invictus* and *Victoria* are also represented on the labari carved on the Arch of Constantine itself in Rome. It is as if the last of the great pagan conceptions were carried on into Christianity, says Altheim.

For our part we would recall that, apart from Constantine, images of the Roman period exist in which the Crucifix itself is surmounted by solar symbols. Altheim notes, however, that a change in outlook was taking place. Now the solar symbol occupies only a subordinate position. The Sun God is no longer the supreme, sovereign God of the Universe, whose reflection is the Imperial universality of Rome. He has become subject and servant to a loftier divinity, the God of the Christians. Altheim thinks, however, that he can point to a pagan antecedent of this new presentation, for in the speculations of the Neoplatonists, and most especially Porphyry, the sun no longer represented the supreme principle. The sun is indeed dominant and a celestial hypostasis, but subordinate to the One; it is the mediator between the One and the manifest world.

To us, however, it seems that we are justified in speaking neither of a real antecedent of the concept adopted by the Christian Emperor, nor of decisive influences exercised by Neoplatonism (Porphyry and Plotinus were among the declared and conscious adversaries of Christianity). A clear distinction should, indeed, be drawn between the point of view of ritual symbolism and that of metaphysical speculation. Only from the first of these points of view could the sun take its place in worship as the supreme principle, for it was considered only as a symbol, and the real reference was to the sovereign and abstract principle of pure light. Very different is the situation with respect to speculations that develop into a cosmology, as with Neoplatonism, in which the matter at issue is a world system, and the sun takes its place in a cosmic hierarchy under symbolic aspects different from those relating to its cult as real celestial Being.

Thus, if relics — one might say echoes — of the "solar spirituality" existed in primitive Christianity (just as the first Patristic
writings, more especially the Greek, preserved many notions
proper to pagan mysteriosophy) one cannot speak of continuity.
Rather, a contrast was to grow between two worlds, two visions
of life and of religion. As the final manifestation of that power
Rome had of stamping her own shape on what was foreign to
her — the power of which Altheim speaks — one may, at most,
point to the phenomenon of the Romanization of early Christianity in several aspects of Catholicism. It was thus that Dante
was able to speak of the Rome for which "Christ is a Roman."
But even so the antithesis, more or less latent, still existed. It was
to make itself clearly manifest in the Middle Ages of the Ghibel-
lines, in which, among other things, it is interesting to note the
reappearance, here and there, of "solar" symbols in the attributes and emblems of the Imperial Party.

East & West, vol. 8, no. 3 (1957): pp. 303–306

THE JAPANESE *HARA* THEORY
& ITS RELATIONS TO
EAST & WEST

On first receiving Karlfried Graf von Dürckheim's book, *Hara, the Terrestrial Center of Man*,[1] we had thought of writing one of the usual reviews, calling attention to it as an interesting contribution to our knowledge of the psychology, behavior, and "existential morphology" of the Far Eastern, more specifically Japanese man. Indeed, in one respect it is a development of things already set forth by the same author in a previous work of a more general character dealing with Japan.[2]

Dürckheim offers us a case parallel to that of Eugen Herrigel, author of a well-known and valuable little book, *Zen in the Art of Archery*.[3] Like Herrigel, he is a German scholar who went to Japan at first with a program of academic studies but was led during his sojourn there to identify himself with his environment and to get into direct touch with spiritual and initiatic traditions that still survive there. These traditions are, above all, the source of the material set forth in Dürckheim's new book.

However, after carefully examining this work, it seemed to us that the main subject is deserving of fuller treatment, both because the matter is almost unknown to the general public,

---

[1] K. Dürckheim, *Hara, die Erdmitte des Menschen* (Munich-Planegg: O. W. Barth-Verlag, 1956), *Hara: The Vital Center of Man*, trans. Sylvia-Monica von Kospoth (Rochester, Vt.: Inner Traditions, 2004).

[2] *Japanund die Kultur der Stille* (Munich-Planegg: O. W. Barth-Verlag, 1954), *The Japanese Cult of Tranquillity*, trans. Samuel Weiser (London: Rider & Co., 1960).

[3] In addition to the German edition published by the same House, this book has appeared in a French and in an Italian translation (Turin: Rigois, 1956). *Zen in the Art of Archery*, trans. R. F. C. Hull (New York: Vintage, 1999).

and because the problems connected with it, especially some of
the questions formulated by the author, also involve the problem of the diverse attitudes assumed in relation to the spirit,
and the task of human reintegration, as seen by the East and
the West. Moreover, some technical questions are touched on,
falling within the field usually thought related to Yoga, which,
considering the attention now paid to it by the West, will perhaps not be without interest for many readers.

The central point of reference of Dürckheim's work is the
Japanese concept of *hara*. In addition to the explanation and
interpretation given by the author, the book contains extracts of
the doctrines of three Japanese masters of modern times —
Okada Torajiro, Sato Tsuji, and Kaneko Shoseki. It is regrettable that the schools to which they belong are not clearly stated,
for as we shall see one of the problems that arises is the question of the origins of the doctrine of *hara*, in light of its special
character which hardly corresponds to the teachings of other
traditions — Asian and non-Asian — on similar subjects.

The doctrine of *hara* cannot but strike a Westerner at first
glance as decidedly eccentric, for strictly speaking it might be
defined as the doctrine of the importance, not only ethical-
existential but also mystical and initiatic, of the belly, or rather
of the lower belly. The literal meaning of *hara* is, indeed, "belly." Another word used also in this connection, *tanden*, denotes
an area of the body "about 4 centimeters below the navel." Yet
another word, used always in the same connection, *koshi*, denotes the lower part of the trunk, from the navel downwards.

The fundamental idea of the doctrine in question is that this
is the zone in which resides not only the basic strength of the
life of the body, but also the primordial unity of man; and that
it is therefore the natural basis of all truly "centralized" human
types, or that which must first of all be secured in carrying out
the existential reintegration of man. Hence we have, on the one
hand, *hara* as a natural fact, and on the other *hara* as the object
of a special discipline.

A chapter, written by Dürckheim on the basis of data collected by a Japanese collaborator, Prof. Fumio Hashimoto, shows
how this concept is reflected in current linguistic usage, which

strikes a European as very strange. For instance, to act or think with *hara*—literally with the belly, *hara de kangaeru*—means to think or act thoroughly, like a whole man, a truly "centered" one. *Hara no aru hito* or *hara no nai hito* means literally a man who has or has not a belly, but it also means a man with a center, or a man without a center, unstable, slippery. Many other interesting examples of curious locutions are adduced.

Considerations on general somatic behavior follow. The Westerner is centered upward; more especially the type considered "virile" holds the head erect, the shoulders are thrown back, the chest forward, the belly drawn in. On the contrary, in the Far Eastern type the upper part of the body is relaxed, the line of the shoulders slopes Raglan-wise, the body centers in the lower portion, in the *hara*.

This is so even in the case of soldiers and wrestlers. Dürckheim points out that this includes the Sumo masters of wrestling. They give an impression of obesity and heaviness, because the seat of their strength is placed low; but at the same time they possess a truly feline agility and swiftness of spring.

Here is another observation: if you give a sudden push to a Westerner he will nearly always fall on the ground because he is "centered upward." It would be much more difficult to do this to an Easterner, because his center of gravity is below.

Next come considerations referring to the inner man. First of all there are the views held by the schools such as Zen, a form of Buddhism related to Taoism, to which the special theory of *hara* is added. From this standpoint, to have *hara* is to dispose of an efficient super-individual strength which is obtained when one succeeds in excluding the direct intervention of the Ego. It is more than physical strength, it is a strength which starts not from the Ego but from the "center."

And here an order of ideas intervenes of a nature more or less well-known to those familiar with disciplines of the Far East. It is the Buddhist theory of the "absence of the Ego," and the Taoist conception of "acting without acting" and of the "void" as signs of a perfection which, in this case however, is not an abstraction but also gives practical evidence of itself in the range of the most varied human activities.

It is said that when a man really has *hara* he does not need physical strength; indeed, he has no need to act himself. It is another mysterious strength that acts for him: without effort, in a natural, sure, and perfect manner, and, in the case of physical conflict, it is irresistible. When the *hara* is not natural but is the result of a discipline followed to obtain it, all tension must be abolished; the individual desire and ambition to succeed must be excluded as well as the fear and anxiety of failure; one must exclude, in short, all intrusion of the Ego. Then an energy that can act much better than the most concentrated will and the most intense effort will make itself manifest.

It is thus that in the several arts, as in wrestling and archery, but also in painting and in the crafts and suchlike, that perfect skill acquires in the Far East a symbolic value. The master of the art becomes such by realizing a different existential dimension, by a spiritual fact to which his mastery bears witness.

As we have said, the specific and singular feature of this ensemble is, however, the literal reference to the *hara*, to the lower belly. Being centered on the lower belly is supposed to be the key. It is said that in their highest forms the way of the tea, the way of the knight, and of the warrior (*budo*), the way of art (*gedo*), the way of sitting and contemplating (*sado*), just as the way of drawing the bow or using the sword, are all ancient arts of the belly (*haragei*), or they are at least related to that art.

In particular, he who has *hara*, even when he acts, moves, and struggles, "does not really move." Hence, an ethical extension of the order of ideas in question. Dürckheim uses in this connection an image from Meister Eckhart: the door may even slam, but the hinge does not move. Hara thus becomes synonymous with inner firmness, the impossibility of any circumstances of life shaking the inmost self.

As is well known, one of the purposes of Zen, when associated with Bushido, with the life of the Samurai, was not to stifle but to existentially destroy the fear of death. Having let the ego fall and having shifted and anchored your center in the "base," the *hara* makes itself felt in the military, as in other fields in natural heroism, quite free from *pathos*, stridency, or sentimentality. Very probably the Kamikaze, the suicide bombing pilots of the last World War, a phenomenon which Westerners find difficult to understand, is not unrelated to the effects of hereditary formation along these lines in Japanese man.

So far we have considered the theory of *hara* affecting a specific type of man, existential behavior, the arts, and ethics. We must now examine a loftier sphere, the purely spiritual one having to do with training of a Yogic and initiatory type. It is here more especially that both the information contained in Dürckheim's book, and what is available in the extracts published in it from the teachings of the Japanese masters themselves, give rise to some perplexity.

One of these masters, Okada, begins by distinguishing three types of men. The first is centered in the head, who, as such, may be said to be decentralized, unstable, "like a pyramid turned upside down." Spirituality for him is nothing but the accumulation of knowledge. Then comes the type centered in the region of the heart, who is compared to one who tries by an individual effort to discipline himself, who struggles with himself, and masters himself. But he does not yet possess real strength. Superior to all these are those men who are centered in the lower belly. "The lower belly is the most important region, the fortress in which divinity may grow, the chamber of the divine. Such men have developed both the body and mind in the right way. They radiate strength, creating the spiritual disposition needed for a higher detachment. Without violating laws, they do all that they wish to do."

Another Master, Sato Tsuji, says that the *tanden* (*hara*) is "the center of man as a unity." "From the physical standpoint it is the center that holds together the body of flesh. In its human significance it is, indeed, also a point, but it should be understood as the original source of strength and not as a point that can be anatomically identified. It is the seat of life, materially ungraspable, which must be experienced internally by the subject himself." It must be made the solid cornerstone on which all else, body and spirit, rests.

Let us quote from a third Master, Kaneko Shoseki. The *hara* is for him "the center of the body where the Origin resides." He says: "What belongs to the head and to the heart is already on the outer edge and therefore far from the essence." "When all the outwardly-directed activities of the mind—representation, judgment, feeling, willpower, in short, all physical energies—are calmly collected in the center of the body, in the *tanden*, then a sphere of perception opens entirely above the opposition of subject and object, outer and inner, and therefore also above the ordinary fluctuating consciousness." When consciousness is transferred to that seat, he adds, "that which alone rules is the universal, primordial force of life, which, as through an iron pipe, flows swiftly and whirls from eternity to eternity, in the lower part of the body."

On this basis, for the realization of this goal of the reintegration of man in the One, or the realization of the Absolute One, various practices are considered, some of the Yoga kind, for they make use of breathing, the position of the body, and of a special form of concentration. To all this we will only make a brief reference. Breathing in the ordinary man is dispersed and decentralized, frequent and irregular, it no longer reaches the *hara*: by subtilizing it, slowing it down (less than 10 breaths per minute) it must again be brought into contact with the *hara*, detaching it, so to say, from the Ego and from all its efforts. One will then experience what may be described as a rebirth of breathing, which regenerates physically and spiritually.

In the matter of concentration. one must get accustomed to accumulating all one's strength in the region of the *hara*, the *tanden*, or the *koshi*—which, as said above, are more or less equivalent expressions. Sato Tsuji says: "The strength with which the *koshi* is filled must be a strength that acts as though the upper part of the body was non-existent. So the energy of the whole body must be gathered in the base of the trunk, as if the vertical body had sprung from the center of the earth."

This is more or less associated with the *seiza*, or art of sitting motionless, a practice for which we have evidence in several ancient Chinese and Japanese schools, given as "a path for transforming the spirit and the body." In this practice, it is said, "one must not struggle to drive away thoughts, but keep awake, holding one's strength in the lower belly." *Seiza* means "the relinquishment of one's own Ego." "Some believe that *seiza* is a form of trance. But, *seiza* means instead to become such that one will no longer be subject to any hypnotic power, however great." If it is rightly practiced, it will reveal the true figure of man, and the false Ego will be eliminated, "To sit in the right way and to think of the true figure" is like bringing to light, little by little, the statue which is already contained in the block of wood" (Sato Tsuji).

Here too the regulation of breathing is of great importance: "*ninjutsu* itself, the art of rendering oneself invisible, and other arts of ancient times, are derived from the mastery of breathing," breathing with the *hara* (Okada Torajiro). The vertical position of the body becomes the act of standing erect, i.e., the vertical arrangement, of the whole being. From this arise "both detached calm and daring strength." The general experience of man is then transformed in the sign of the Great One. An eternal springtime is felt in this world, everywhere, in heaven and on earth.

We have now given the essential points of the Japanese doctrine of *hara* and of all connected with it. Let us now see what position we should take towards it. Seen from the more external point of view, related to somatic behavior and morphological anthropology, the man with *hara*, i.e., centered and developed in the lower part of his body, can evidently only be considered as a specifically Far Eastern type.

Dürckheim, who would like to attach general human importance to the *hara* theory, believes that the human type to which it refers, while it is in complete antithesis to the physical ideal of the modern Westerner, has in other ages been considered normal in Europe also. In his book, which contains several illustrations, he offers in proof of this some figures from Gothic statues in which the lower part of the body is considerably developed or in relief, and compares them with similar figures from the statuary of the Far East. We do not think, however, that this kind of thing can be taken seriously.

We may ascribe solely to more recent Western civilization the human type centered unilaterally on the upper portion of the body, the chest thrust forward, the broad shoulders and stomach held in, as though to emphasize physical individuality and the Ego. But even in other periods, the prevailing somatic ideal of the West, starting from that of the Hellenes, has been distinctly different from that of the Far East. To say that to be centered in the head is "contrary to the order of life," while to be centered low down, in the *hara*, is in keeping with it, is an idea which cannot be valid beyond a very limited area.

If we limit ourselves to the symbolic level, we could find in China an antecedent of the Japanese theory of the *hara*. The Chinese images of divinities, the Buddha, and sages, in which the stomach is particularly pronounced, are well known. This has a purely symbolic value. The belly, indeed, was held to be the "empty" part of the body, as compared to the remaining portions. Thus, the figure with a big belly is supposed to express symbolically a being who has developed the "void," and has made it predominate over the "full."

Here the "void" stands for the metaphysical principle of the super-substantial "Non-Being" that conditions Being, spoken of by Lao-tzu and Mahayana Buddhism, which was imported into China and mixed with Taoism. In Lao-tzu (Tao Te Ching, 12) we read, "Shih i sheng jen wei fu wei mu" (The sage is for the belly and not for the eye), that is to say, he does not turn to the reality revealed by external experience (to "seeing") but to the essential principle.

However, as we have seen, the Japanese doctrine of *hara* is not mere symbolism, and we may also exclude the idea that it is derived from a gross materialistic interpretation of the symbolic content discussed. We have indeed seen that the *hara*, the *tanden*, and the *koshi* are spoken of as a definite part of the body, physically and occultly considered, which has a clearly defined place in practices of a Yogic type. We have here a doctrine to which it is not easy to find anything that truly corresponds, not only in Western traditions but even in those of other Oriental civilizations.

The *hara*, taken not only in a physical sense, is called both the center of man in general, and the earth-center of man (this is the literal subtitle of Dürckheim's book[4]) and also the seat of

---

[4] "die Erdmitte des Menschen," i.e., the terrestrial center of man — Eds.

the One, the "basic center," designations which do not fully agree one with the other. In the first place, "to be centered" and "to be centered below" are evidently not synonyms. It would be more logical to place the center in a median zone of the psychophysical being. It is for this reason that in the concordant traditions of West and East, the heart, taken in a non-physical sense, has been considered as the center of being. This doctrine, as is well known, is specially attested in the Upanishads; nor is it absent from the secret and mystical traditions of the West and of Islam. In other cases, it has been the solar plexus, likewise not considered in a solely physical sense, to which the meaning of "center" of man and of human life has been attributed. It would thus seem that by the doctrine of *hara* as "center," one abnormal and unilateral dislocation (upwards, towards the head) has been replaced by another of the same kind (downwards, in the belly), and in this case one could not speak of a real centrality, of the *hara* as the "middle center." Moreover, the expression "basic center" is misleading, as the connotations of "base" and of "center" or "middle point" are different.

A hint given by Sato Tsuji that the head is Heaven and *hara* the Earth, and that it is a question of actuating the "void" of heaven and the "fullness" (plenitude) of Earth by means of the practices spoken of before, is interesting but does not adequately clarify the problem.

Another difficulty is that the "seat of the One" and "center of the earth," of "strength" or of "Life," cannot be identified, either. The Tantric Yoga doctrine about the hyper-physical structure of the body contains some teachings that might be approximated to those concerning *hara*. That doctrine speaks indeed of the "basic center," *muladhara*, which is placed in relation to the earth, *protivi*, and is considered as the seat of Shakti, the power or life of the One, under the form of *kundalini*. Symbols of stability and weight are also mentioned, expressed by the square and by the elephant.[5]

---

[5] See the reproductions of Hindu miniatures of the *chakra* in Arthur Avalon, *The Serpent Power*. Cf. my *The Yoga of Power*.

But these parallels are very imperfect. In the first place, the *muladhara* is situated at the base of the spinal column, whereas the *hara* is just below the navel. Second, the center dealt with is the seat of Shakti, of life or power, and not of the One. According to Tantric Yoga, the Absolute One is achieved not at the base but at the summit of the head, in the *sahasrara chakra*, where the reawakened Shakti joins and merges completely with the opposite principle, Shiva, the eternal male. And the Yoga process of the descent of consciousness into the inner part of the hyper-physical corporeality, to come into contact with Shakti and reawaken *kundalini*, is openly subordinated to this ascending process. But above all it should be noted that in Hindu metaphysics, Shakti is considered to be the principle of movement and change—not of stability and immutability, that is to say of "centrality," which is assigned instead to Shiva or to another analogous principle of the *purushic* type. Shakti corresponds to "Life," not to "Being."

It may, however, be objected that the comparison with the ideas of Hindu metaphysics is not suitable because of its inherent dualism; that a more suitable comparison could be made, if any, with the ideas of Chinese metaphysics, more especially with those of Taoism, which have as their background what might be termed an "immanent transcendence." However, if we refer to the secret Taoist doctrines, we find that they are nearer to those of the Hindus than to those of the Japanese.

In the process of spiritual regeneration, called sometimes the formation of the Golden Flower of the Great One, sometimes the creation of the immortal embryo, special importance is given to the lower part of the body, but the value of basis or center is not assigned to it. It corresponds to the *yin* aspect of the body and of being, and the whole process—whatever be the means used, breathing or something else—always follows the pattern of the junction of opposites, of the *yang* and the *yin*, for this alone leads to the One.

As *yang* corresponds to heaven, *yin* to earth, one might also draw a comparison with *hara*, where *hara* is defined as "the center of the earth." A further correspondence might exist between *hara* as the center of strength and the *yin* region of the body (which is that below the diaphragm), known also as the "Field of the Lower Cinnabar," because this is also held to be "the space of strength." In the secret Taoist doctrine, it is indeed considered essential to reach this region, crossing a threshold "which the gods do not open lightly," but the process does not end there. The last stage is an ascending one in which the "Field of the Upper Cinnabar" is attained and the "center of the brain" is regenerated. Here is located the Palace of Ni-huan (the Chinese transcription of the Sanskrit word *nirvana*), and until the time of the Han dynasty the Great One was also placed there. The scheme is thus similar to that of Hindu Yoga.[6]

An inquiry into the doctrine of the "center" in the West would indeed be of much interest for the purposes of a further comparison. However, this presents special difficulties because esoteric knowledge in the West has taken the form of cryptograms, and has been clothed in abstruse symbols and myths of many meanings to which a uniform interpretation, such as modern critical thought desires, cannot always be given. We shall therefore only make a few references.

The ancient traditions about the sacred stone, the *betilos*, are well known. It had the meaning of a "center," and was known to Rome under the name of *abadir*. The etymological derivation of *betilos* from *"beth-el"* or "house of God," is not to be excluded.[7] This was also the name given by Jacob to the stone he used as a pillow when, in his well-known dream, he had the vision of the house of God and of the gates of Heaven. It was, moreover, the name given by Jacob to the town near the place of his dream. Now, certain Western esoteric doctrines, of Kabbalistic origin, have developed these symbols into a theory of the basic center.

---

[6] See the material collected by Henri Maspero, "Les procédés de nourrir l'esprit vital dans la religion taoïste ancienne," *Journal Asiatique,* Vol. 229 (April–June, July–September, 1937). In addition, the *T'ai I Chin hua Taung chih,* translated in more than one European language under the title *The Secret of the Golden Flower,* and also again Maspero, *Le Taoïsme* (Paris: Civilisation du Sud, 1950), pp. 110–11, 115, etc.

[7] Cf. René Guénon, *The King of the World,* trans. Henry D. Fohr (Hillsdale, NY: Sophia Perennis, 2001).

Thus, referring to the fact that in Genesis the original name of Beth-el was Luz, it has been noted that *luz* is the Hebrew name of an "indestructible osselet," in which the words "bone" and "indestructible" have been used in an allegorical sense, not material but spiritual. Agrippa says that "from it, like a plant from a seed, the human body sprouts again in the resurrection of the dead—and this quality is not ascertained by reasoning but by experience."[8]

But the fact is that in Aramaic "luz" is precisely the bone attached to the lower end of what is curiously enough known as the "sacrum," at the base of the spinal column, that is to say precisely at the place where the Hindu Tantric Yogic teaching locates the basic center, the *muladhara*. The religious concept of the "resurrection of the dead" is homologated in this exegesis with the initiatic idea of spiritual reintegration (note Agrippa's reference to the fact that it is a question of a matter of experience—inner experience). Lastly, there is the idea, which is always part of the same tradition, that in the vicinity of Luz access was to be found for reaching a symbolic hidden city, one in which "the Angel of Death cannot enter nor have over it any power."[9] All this might lead us to an order of ideas similar to that of the esoteric doctrine of the *hara* as basic center.

It is difficult to give evidence, in the secret Western traditions, of the precise location of the lower center in terms of hyperphysical anatomy, because it is likely that this knowledge has not had in the West the development that characterizes the Hindu and Far Eastern doctrines. One of the few existing documents is the work of a disciple of Boehme, Johann Georg Gichtel, which appeared in 1696 under the title *Theosophia practica*. This work is illustrated by several colored plates, the work of Johann Georg Graber, which refer to the occult constitution of fallen man and of regenerated man. They show a zone of the

---

[8] *De Occulta Philosophia*, I. 20, *Three Books of Occult Philosophy Written by Henry Cornelius Agrippa*, trans. James Freake (London: Rider & Co., 1960).

[9] For references on this matter see the collective work *Introduzione alla Magia* (Milan: Bocca, 1955), vol. I., pp. 115, 141.

body which might correspond approximately to the *hara*, as it is placed in the lower part, but centering in the genitals. The plates showing unregenerate man bear the inscription: "the dark world, the root of the souls in the center of Nature." Thus, we find that the idea of a basic center (root-center) — "center of Nature" in the language of Boehme — is more or less equivalent to the "center of the Earth" in the language of the Far East. In another plate we find attached to this zone the words "Hell, Satan."

However, in the doctrine as a whole set forth by Gichtel, a doctrine which certainly brings together elements of previous experiences and traditions, it would seem that this dark and infernal character is not intrinsic to the lower center, that it is only referred to as the manner in which the primordial principle, the *Urgrund*, of the divine manifests itself in fallen man, and that it is only necessary to effect a certain transformation in that center to bring about the regeneration of man, the union of the principles of "Light" and "Fire" which were disassociated by the Fall. Let us quote these two passages from Gichtel:

> Below the heart, where (in Living Man) the divine Light of the World resides, there is the divine, magic eye of marvels, and the Fire, which in the regenerate is the place where the Father generates the Son, who is in the heart. In the others it is the Fire of Divine Wrath. It is the bottom of Heaven and of Hell, and of the visible world whence come good and evil, as also light and darkness, life and death, blessedness and damnation. . . . It is called the *Mysterium Magnum* because it contains two beings and two wills.

The lower part of the body is therefore referred, as in the doctrine of *hara*, to a primordial, non-dual principle — but one with an ambivalent character. However, the palingenesis conceived by Gichtel is not completed in the lower seat, but rather in the higher one, more especially in the heart, from which a vinculum is removed, symbolized by a serpent coiled round the sign of the Sun. It is the vinculum of the Ego — and a light is lit which is the principle of the palingenesis of the body and of the formation of the "perfect, angelic man." The correspondence with the theory of *hara* is therefore only partial.

We find a last indication in the illustrations to the work of Robert Fludd, *Utriusque Cosmi Historia* (Oppenheim, 1619), in which the human body is inserted in circles pointing to the correspondences between macrocosm and microcosm. The center of these circles is in the lower part of the body, more or less in the genitals, where we find inscribed *"Centrum."* Something similar is found in Agrippa[10] and in other writers of the same esoteric trend. The anonymous text *De Pharmaco Catholico* speaks in symbols of an "infernal niter" which is a "fiery magic key" with the power to destroy a principle which seems to allude, through the symbols used, to the exterior and individual Ego.

It should be noted in considering all this, however, that the *hara* is not placed in the genitals, and that there is no reference in the Far Eastern doctrine to the secret power of sex, which seems in this way to have been taken into consideration by the Western theories, and which is also not absent in the Tantric theory of the *muladhara* and the *kundalini*. Therefore, the *hara* doctrine, as compared to similar traditions, including Asian ones, offers features of its own, which give rise to the problem of its origin and its foundations.

As a matter of principle, the subject with which we are dealing should, in a certain sense, be objective. It has always been thought that what may be called "spiritual corporeality" is not a matter of opinion but of knowledge; it would therefore seem that there should be no more differing views on the subject than there are on the anatomy and physiology of the physical body, which do not differ in men of different races and civilizations.

Should the divergences now mentioned be real, and not due to imperfect information or formulation, one might indeed wonder if they are not accounted for by a difference in the man of the Far East, not only in his existential attitudes but also in

---

[10] *Theosophia practica*, II. 6; IV, pp. 18–20.

his hyperphysical structure. This difference would then account for the diversity in the methods of spiritual realization.

In everything that we have said till now, we have referred above all to what can be deduced from the extracts of Japanese teachings published in Dürckheim's book. It will be suitable to add a few words about what the author himself has to say, for he has not only explained and described the doctrine of *hara* but, with the enthusiasm of a neophyte, has become its apologist and, as we have noted, has seen fit to attribute to it universal validity, making it therefore applicable to Western man: this most ancient path, that of *hara*, would thus also be a new one, to be used for "a decisive task of our time" (p. 183), for a necessary rectification of a decentralization of which Western man is above all guilty, and from which he is suffering.

We shall deal later with this last point. For the moment we will note that the framework in which Dürckheim has placed the doctrine of *hara* makes it in part more acceptable. We would again remind the reader that the problem does not involve the general views held by Zen, and by similar schools, on the liberation from the Ego, on finding centralization and an invulnerable stability, on acquiring the capacity to "act without acting." All this raises no difficulty. Instead, the question is that of the specific relation established between these spiritual aims and Eastern practice directed towards *hara*, with the corresponding emphasis on the importance of the lower part of the body. Dürckheim attenuates the specific and drastic character of this doctrine, for he speaks also, though not without inconsistencies, of a higher dimension of the whole process. He quotes the proverb: "You cannot win heaven if you neglect the earth, if you do not first say yes to the earth," and he sees in this what is meant by transporting one's center to the *hara*. This transfer would then have (as in the Hindu and Chinese teachings referred to above) the meaning of a simple preliminary stage. "The *hara*," he says on page 123, "reveals the terrestrial center of being but not yet the celestial center." In a certain sense, the transfer to the *hara* would make it possible to cast off the spell of the ego; it would enable the deeper vital forces from which man has detached himself to rise within him in order to free him and shape him.

We are reminded that "every real ascent into the spirit is preceded by a descent into the center of the earth." This indeed is a teaching held in common by many traditions both of the East and of the West. On the religious plane it has given rise to the symbolism of Christ descending into Hell before ascending into Heaven, and to that of Dante's journey in *The Divine Comedy*.

Parallel and more specific symbols are given, as noted by Dürckheim (without, however, adequately elaborating the corresponding features) by the Western doctrine of hermetic alchemy. A well-known formula of this tradition, ascribed to Basilius Valentinus, is that of the anagram VITRIOLUM, interpreted as *Visita Interiora Terrae Rectifi cando Invenies Occultum Lapidem Veram Medicinam*.[11] Here again the idea is that of a descent to the center of the earth to find the Philosopher's Stone, the real medicine, i.e., the principle of the reintegration of the human being.[12]

However, it remains to be seen whether the specific doctrine of *hara* can be placed within this wider framework. We have, indeed, already pointed out the difference between the several definitions of *hara* understood in a non-material sense. *Hara* is not only called the center of the earth, the dark zone of the depths, but it is also the "casket of the divine," "the seat of the One," even the seat of a superior unity and of the "non-dual state." This means that an absolute value is given to it, the value of a totality.

Dürckheim himself is constantly alternating between one of these meanings and the other; now he sees in *hara* the center of primordial unconscious life, now (as at page 113) the seat of transcendence, for it is there that contact is made with the "überweltlichen Kräften seines Wesens" (otherworldly powers of Being). It would therefore seem difficult to deprive the doc-

---

[11] "Visit the interior of the earth, and by rectifying (what you find there) you will find the hidden stone which is the true medicine" — Eds.

[12] *De occulta philosophia*, IL, p. 27.

trine of *hara*, taken as a whole, of its character as a kind of monistic doctrine of a power centered in the lower regions, centered, that is to say, more towards "Life" and the "Earth" than towards "Being," or the true totality.

If we turn to the message that the teaching and the path of *hara* may offer to the Westerner, some precise reservations must be made. One may, of course, condemn the artificial and unilateral "upward centralization" not of the Western man in particular but of the West of modern times, a centralization corresponding to the prevalence of the cerebral and purely individual Ego with no deep roots. But one must take care that a reaction to this does not lead us to that irrationalism and vitalism which has made itself felt in many branches of our more recent Western culture, ranging from the theories of Bergson to those of Klages on the "mind as the antagonist of the soul," from the views of Spengler to those of psychoanalysis in general, and C. G. Jung in particular.

We are far from sure that Dürckheim is not affected to some extent by this irrationalist attitude. Does he not speak (p. 142) of a leap to be taken "into the sphere of the primordial life acting on the unconscious"? Jung, with his devious theory of archetypes and of a pseudo-process of individual integration, would not express himself otherwise. If thus misinterpreted — and in the West all the assumptions for such a misinterpretation are present — the doctrine of *hara* might lead to a reversed integration, to a dissolution of the Ego, not into what lies above the individual finite consciousness — the true Transcendency, the Absolute One — but into that which is below it — "Life," the subconscious, the reign of the "Mother," the Freudian "Id."

The campaign of the irrationalists and of the psychoanalysts against the fictitious Ego, split and full of tensions, is indeed a function of this regressive direction: and it is a real nuisance that Jung was entrusted with the task of writing introductions to a number of Oriental and Western esoteric and mystical works, including of those of Zen and the text of the *Secret of the Golden Flower*, with a view to explaining them and "giving them scientific value" by interpreting them along the lines of his doctrine of the "unconscious." But when Dürckheim speaks of a return to "Universal Life," we seem to recognize this same irrationalist pathos of the mysticism of Life, although he often speaks also of transcendence.

If the Ego, more especially in the Westerner, fears, as Dürckheim says, to take a leap into the sphere of primordial life and of the unconscious, this is not without existential reasons. As we have referred to the hermetic teachings about the descent into the lower regions of being, a descent related to the phase of "dissolution" (the Nigredo, or "Operation of the Black" in technical terminology), it will be well to refer also to the other teaching of the same tradition, according to which this spiritual adventure — not free from risks — should be undertaken only by those who possess what the text-books call "the grain of gold," the "incombustible sulfur," or the "spermatic seed." These expressions allude to a principle which can overcome the crisis of dissolution and arise again in a subsequent stage, which is that of real reintegration.[13]

Now, it may be supposed that the modern Westerner is badly lacking in this principle, and it is for this reason that, so far as he possesses a certain equilibrium, he instinctively fears to plunge into the "obscurity of the formless One, in order to reach the light" (p. 132), having good reasons for this fear. The existential atmosphere of the Western world in general is entirely unfavorable to adventures of that kind, and for this reason it is not desirable that doctrines of an esoteric character, such as those referred to, should be divulged in the West. They might give rise to the delusion that they could be used for the purposes of a general process of recovery, when, as a matter of fact, they can only have beneficial effects for an exiguous number of exceptionally qualified persons.

Matters stand otherwise in the East, both as the result of a different heredity and because of the survival of schools, traditions, and institutions, and also perhaps because of that different structure of the "non-physical corporeality" which we men-

---

[13] On hermetic doctrines, see our *The Hermetic Tradition: Symbols and Teachings of the Royal Art*, trans. E. E. Rehmus (Rochester, Vt.: Inner Traditions, 1995).

tioned as a hypothesis to explain some anomalous aspects of the theory of *hara*. The valid element of this theory is perhaps limited to the general task of creating a "centered" human type, possessing as such a sound basis and calm strength; free from both an excess and a lack of the Ego; from egocentric rigidness and from vulnerability to vital and irrational forces. The task, however, is one which, in the case of the Westerner, will have to be fulfilled in a specific form in keeping with his tradition and with the finer factors that condition him.

East & West, vol. 9, nos. 1–2 (March–June, 1958): pp. 76–84

THE "MYSTERIES OF WOMAN" IN EAST & WEST

In this essay, the "Mysteries of Woman" means those traditions which refer to a female principle and the participation of man in its worship in multiple forms, whether they be those of spiritual exaltation, enlightenment, or real initiation. As a rule, the starting point is a divine hypostasis, a female divinity or "occult" woman, conceived as being the ontological principle made manifest in real women who therefore contain it in themselves, and are its potential bearers. The "feminine mysteries" may therefore present two forms. In one of them the endeavor is to enter directly into contact with "woman in herself," with the "divine woman"; in the other, this contact is always the essential aim, but the starting point is found in a real woman and in the emotions she awakens, and sexual union itself may be considered as the means to the participation. Here we shall only consider some typical cases of the "feminine mysteries," so as to draw a comparison between Western and Eastern traditions. The field of our enquiry will necessarily be restricted; yet it will illustrate clearly enough the convergence or parallelism of some of the fundamental themes. The ancient civilizations of the Mediterranean area can offer us much material of importance, connected with the cult of she who was known as the Great Goddess. We shall, however, only glance at this branch of the history of religions for the purpose of a few rapid references. The Egyptian and Assyrian figures so frequently found of a goddess or divine woman offering the "key of life," or the "beverage of life," evidently express the central theme of the Mysteries of Woman. In the ancient civilization of Crete, the goddess herself was often undistinguished from her priestesses, and there is reason to believe that the cult intended for the former was often transferred to the latter as her incarnations.[1] However, one of the

---

[1] See Gustave Glotz, *La civilisation égéenne* (Turin: Einaudi, 1954), pp.

most typical forms is that of the so-called "sacred prostitution" practiced in many of the ancient temples dedicated to the Great Goddess: Ishtar, Mylitta, Aphrodite, Anaitis, Innini, etc. In those temples there was a permanent body of *hierodules*: of women in the service of the Goddess who celebrated the mystery of carnal love in order to transmit, as it were through an efficient sacrament, the influence or virtue to those with whom they joined, evoking the Goddess in them. Also, these young women were thought to be in a certain way incarnations of the divine woman. They were called "sacred virgins" (*parthenoi ierai*), beings pure and sacred: *qadishtu, mugig, zermasitu*, expressions which evidently are not to be taken as referring to the values of the profane world but to those of their specific religious function.[2] We will not linger here on the part that woman played in the cult of Dionysus.

The Platonic conception of *eros* is well known as the principle of a sacred exaltation (*mania*) which was compared to that of the initiates in the Mysteries. It is probable that in its origin this theory was connected with the Mysteries of Woman, an echo of which is likely to have survived also in the Eleusinian Mysteries. However, as treated by Plato it acquires an abstract character, for in the end it refers to the spiritual exaltation and the ecstatic rapture aroused by Beauty *per se*, not by the beauty of any special being, still less by some individual woman. Nevertheless, in Plato the connection between a given type of *eros* and participation in immortality is stated. One of the bases on which this idea rests is the Platonic doctrine of the androgyne, itself derived from the Mysteries, which in the West continued to be professed in more or less underground currents, in Hermetism, in the Kabbalah, and even in some Christian mystics.[3] In these currents the theme of the spiritual reintegration of fallen man through the female

---

308, 312; *The Aegean Civilization*, trans. M. R. Dobie & E. M. Riley (London: K. Paul, Trench, Trubner & Co., 1925).

   [2] See S. Langdon, *Tammuz and Ishtar* (Oxford: Clarendon Press, 1914), pp. 80–82.

   [3] E. Benz, *Der Mythus des Urmenschen* (Munich: Otto-Wilhelm-Barth Verlag, 1955), has brought together the leading texts of this last current.

principle frequently recurs, conceived in various forms of which one of the most ancient is Sophia—Wisdom, Gnosis, transcendent Intelligence—of Christian Gnosticism. Jacob Boehme and his disciple Johann Georg Gichtel speak again of Sophia. The same theme was to appear within the framework of Jewish tradition through the so-called Sabbatianism. Jacob Franck in particular defended an esoteric interpretation of the advent of the Messiah, considering it not as a historical or collective event but as the symbol of the awakening of the individual, of the enlightenment which sets free and leads beyond the precepts of the Law. Moreover, he connected the mystic power of the Messiah to a female principle, a transcendent woman present in every woman as the principle and origin of her power.[4] This gave the impetus to forms of erotic mysticism, also with aberrant and orgiastic features, in which some authorities, not without reason, have recognized a revival of the ancient cult of the Great Goddess. Similar revivals, assuming even more distorted and dark forms, are found in medieval demonology and in the Black Mass, whose fundamental theme was a kind of sacrament that centered in a woman, the "Queen of Sheba" and similar figures, and a ritual and evocative character was attributed to the defloration or possession of this woman by the officiating priest.[5] Let us close with a reference to the Russian sect of the Khlysti, whose secret rites, celebrated in common, centered round a young naked woman, sometimes looked on as the Virgin, sometimes as Mother Earth. In an atmosphere of exaltation which culminated in promiscuous sexual intercourse, the participants awaited the descent of the Spirit, and the fulfilment of the "marvelous mystery of the transmutation."[6] These are all echoes of a lost and degraded tradition. The notion of nuptials and direct magical unions with invisible female beings can be found in the sagas of many peo-

---

[4] M. D. Langer, *Die Erotik in der Kabbala* (Prague: Verlag Dr. Josef Flesch, 1923), pp. 30–54.

[5] See M. Murray, *The God of the Witches* (London: S. Low, Marston & Co., 1933); S. De Guaita, *Le serpent de la Genese: Le Temple de Satan* (Paris: H. & H. Durville, 1916), vol. I, pp. 154 ff.

[6] See N. Tsakni, *La Russie sectaire* (Paris: Plon, 1888), Chapter 4, pp. 63–73.

ples and in some of the medieval traditions of magic. It connects also with the so-called *Alpminne* of the German Middle Ages. Paracelsus himself dealt with this subject.

But let us return to Plato to point out that what was called Platonic Love laid the foundations for an important current of medieval thought, of which the true meaning is still known to only a few. It is commonly held that Platonic Love is something purely ideal, romantic, Victorian, shunning all physical contact with woman. All this is but its exterior aspect and is somewhat in the nature of a caricature. Platonic Love is rather a tendency in which the desire and rapture aroused by woman is not allowed to develop along material and profane lines, but is used as the means for a spiritual realization, which may even partake of the nature of an initiation. For such purposes a real woman is simply used as the starting point and as a support. Through her the "Lady of the Mind" is evoked. This Lady is the real object of *eros*, and she is recognized as having the power to awaken in her lover the "new life," to actualize his true nature, to assure his salvation. Much of the chivalrous cult of woman, and of service to woman proper to the Western medieval world, can be traced back to this conception. So also the forms that have arisen from an incomprehension of the original and more profane content of the doctrine are no less significant. The true object of the cult in question was indeed a woman possessed of autonomous reality, apart from the physical personality of the real woman, who could eventually serve as her support, and who could, in a certain sense, incorporate and represent her. It was in the imagination that this Lady lived and had her dwelling; thus it was on a subtle, hyperphysical plane that many knights enacted their desires and raptures. Only thus can one account for the fact that the choice of the Lady to whom the knight dedicated his life, and whom he honored by engaging in all kinds of hazardous undertakings, was often one such that the possibility of really possessing her was excluded from the start; or else she was a Lady inaccessible whose "cruelty" was accepted and even extolled; or she might be the mere image of a Lady who did indeed exist but who the knight had never seen. The expressions *donnoi* or *donnei* were used in some of the circles of Provence to designate a type of erotic relationship from which physical possession was *a priori* excluded.[7] Rilke is not mistaken when he says that in some cases it would seem that what was feared above all else was that courtship might be successful. The fact is that something other and above physical possession was sought, something to which greater value was attached than to the pleasures and emotions of human passion. The idea of "magic nuptials" and of "occult intercourses" seems also to have been at the basis of a rumor concerning the Order of the Templars; it was said that these knights had commerce with demons and that though they practiced chastity, each of them possessed a "Lady" of his own.[8] If the theology discussed in the castles and in the courts of love enjoined fealty both to God and to the lady of the knight's choice, asserting that there could be no doubt as to the spiritual salvation of he who died for the "Lady of his mind," this leads us back again to the "Mysteries of Woman," that is to say to the notion of the immortalizing power that a given type of *eros* can possess.

The "mystery of Platonic Love" of the Middle Ages has been referenced in relation not only to the world of chivalry and of the courts of love in which—as noted—the original and deeper content of the doctrine was often not understood, but also to the Fedeli d'Amore (the Faithful of Love). It has often been thought, and many still think, that these Faithful were only poets. To their number belonged Dante, Guido Cavalcanti, and other early medieval Italian authors. In fact, they were a secret order of initiates whose doctrines deviated widely from those of the Catholic Church and whose experiences were in line with those of the Mysteries of Woman. All this was already known in the West in very exclusive circles, but in modern times the true character of

---

[7] See C. Fauriel, *Histoire de la poesie provencale* (Paris: Labitte, 1846), trans. into English by G. J. Adler, *History of Provençal Poetry* (New York: Derby & Jackson, 1860); P. L. Jacob & F. Kellerhoven, *Moeurs, usages et coutumes au Moyen-Age et l'epoque de la Renaissance* (Paris: Firmin Didot, 1873), trans. into English, *Manners, Customs, and Dress During the Middle Ages, and During the Renaissance Period* (London: Bickers & Son, 1874).

[8] See G. Garinet, *Histoire de la Magie en France* (Paris: Foulon, 1818), p. 292.

the Fedeli d'Amore was revealed by Gabriele Rossetti and later on by Luigi Valli.[9] Certainly the Fedeli d'Amore wrote poetry, but their poetry was of a cryptic character. It dealt with love, but this love was very different from the common variety. The many ladies celebrated by these poets, from Dante onwards, by whatever names they were known, were all the same, the image of Holy Wisdom, of Gnosis, that is to say of a principle of enlightenment, of salvation, of transcendent knowledge. Therefore, it was not a question of personified theological abstraction, as many commentators on Dante had thought in the case of Beatrice, but of the "initiatic woman," the "Lady of the Miracle," the "glorious woman of the mind" (thus Dante calls her and adds: "who was called Beatrix by many who knew no other name to give her"), that is to say, a being, a real efficient power, whose effects have often been described in dramatic form. To behold this Lady, to receive her "salutation," to make love operate, is something that kills, that wounds, that strikes like lightning. At the same time, the Lady bestows salvation (there is often a play of words on the Italian expression "*salute*"; the texts speak of the Lady who "salutes," and this may mean giving her greeting as well as giving salvation = *salute*). *Mors osculi*, death in a kiss, was an earlier Kabbalistic formula. Some among the Fedeli d'Amore speak of a "light which strikes the heart," causing loss of control over the limbs and the vital spirit. But by striking the heart and slaying, "the mind that slumbered is awakened." "From this death, life will arise," writes one of these poets. There are some who, when dealing with the "grades and powers of true love," consider ecstasy *quae dicitur excessus mentis* [what is called being beside oneself], as the climax of them all, and they add: *sicut fuit raptus Paulus* [as Paul was taken]. The experience is thus assimilated to that of which St. Paul speaks.

In relation to the "miraculous Lady of all virtue" (virtue = power) and to the "higher virtue of the nuptials," we should re-

---

[9] G. Rossetti, *Il Mistero dell'amor platonico del Medioevo* (Londra: Dalla tipografia di Riccardo e Giovanni E. Taylor, 1840); L. Valli, *Il linguaggio segreto di Dante e dei Fedeli d'Amore* (Rome: Optima, 1928); A. Ricolfi, *Studi sui Fedeli d'Amore* (Milan: Albrighi, Segati & Co., 1933).

member that Da Barberino also introduces the symbol of the androgyne, i.e., of the One who puts an end to the dual condition of the split individual. Jacob de Baisieux, a Provençal exponent of the same trend of thought, deduces from the word *amor* itself that immortality is the end that is sought. He explains this word thus: *a-mors*: the meaning of *a* is without; *mors* means death, "Amor = without death." The experience is not without problematic, even dangerous, features. Some, indeed, utter the warning cry: "Fly if you are not willing to die." Dante gives to Love personified a "fearful" aspect.

No less interesting is the reference to the intellectual side of such experiences. One of the names by which the Lady is known is "Madonna Intelligenza." She is the Holy Wisdom. Cavalcanti speaks of the "possible intellect" as the place in which Love acts and where the Lady exercises her power. The "possible intellect" is a technical expression from Aristotle's doctrine as interpreted by Averroes. It expresses the *nous*, the transcendent, super-individual, transfiguring intellect which in the ordinary man is a mere potential faculty; it is for this reason that it is called the "possible intellect." Regeneration, or a New Life, is a recurrent motif. The *Vita Nuova* is the title of Dante's famous cryptic work. In the *Convivio* (*The Banquet*) Dante attributes to the "Lady of the Miracle" the power to "renew the nature of those who behold her, which is a marvelous thing." Life in the higher initiatic sense is bestowed by the Woman. Therefore, Cecco d'Ascoli says that his Lady shaped his mind and showed him salvation, and that when union with her is interrupted, he "feels again the darkness of death."[10]

Even these necessarily brief references clearly show that the matter dealt with by the Fedeli d'Amore was something quite other than mere poetry, or sublimated sentimentality and sophisticated symbolism. The experiences they recorded should be traced back to the Mysteries of Woman; they essentially took place on a hyperphysical plane and had an initiatory character.

---

[10] For detailed documentation on this subject see our work *Metafisica del sesso* (Rome: Atanòr, 1958), pp. 262–61; English ed.: *The Metaphysics of Sex* (Rochester, Vt.: Inner Traditions, 1983), pp. 191-202.

The part that real women played in such experiences remains an open question. Interpretation should avoid two extremes, that which would assign to real women and to sublimated human feelings the essential part, and that which sees only symbols when the poets speak of love and of women. The foundations of the *eros* and of the rapture awakened by woman, by the image of woman or by her magnetism, must have been real. The level on which the *eros* acted was, however, something other than the usual one. It would seem that the technique was essentially that of Platonic Love, understood as set forth above. In fact, from all that is known of the Fedeli d'Amore, it would not seem that they also practiced non-Platonic forms of sexual initiation, making a concrete use "even if not a profane and carnal one" of woman, as was the case in the ancient Mediterranean practices to which we have already referred, or of the Oriental ones with which we shall now deal.

Some have thought that, in addition to the Gnostic influences (the notion of Sophia, the female hypostases of Wisdom and of the Holy Spirit, etc.), the Fedeli d'Amore must have been influenced by some aspects of Islamic Sufism. Indeed, a literature did grow up on the margin of Sufism stressing the theme of love, of women, and of ecstasy, but with reference to mystic and spiritual experiences. However, it remains to be seen in what measure many of the expressions used by those poets were also of a positive and not only of a symbolic and mystic nature, with no real relation to sex.

To find Oriental themes and experiences which can best be compared to those with which we have been dealing, we must turn to India. Indeed, in this as in other fields, the Orient offers, in more complete and fully developed forms, that which in the West has often survived only in dim and fragmentary shape.

Already in traditional texts that trace back directly to the *Shruti*, the union between man and woman, had frequently been considered as a true sacrificial rite, as an equivalent to the sacrifice of the fire (*homa*), the woman or her body being assimilated to the fire.[11] In this context the *Satapatha Brahmana* (1, 8–9) puts

---

[11] See the quotations collected by R. L. Mukherji in J. Woodroffe,

the following words in the mouth of the woman: "If thou wilt make use of me at the sacrifice, then whatever blessing thou shalt invoke through me shall be granted." But the more interesting forms are those found in the Tantras, both Hindu (Agama) and Buddhist (Vajrayana and Sahajiya).

The fundamental background of the Tantras is generally considered to be derived from obscure and orgiastic cults proper to the lower aboriginal, pre-Aryan strata of Hindu civilization. From those are derived some dark forms of sexual magic, which, however, if considered in their main structural lines, have features that differ but little from the higher and more elaborate forms. We are thinking of the rites by which it was believed that special powers could be acquired by summoning up female entities—"*yaksini, dakhini, apsara*"—to enter the body of a woman, and then subduing them by forcing and possessing this woman in such wild places as forests or cemeteries.[12] Developments on a higher level than this are found among the Shaktas owing to their introduction of a particular kind of metaphysics. The Shaktas believe that a female being, the *Shakti*, is the supreme principle of the Universe, and they see in every woman the incarnation of this divinity. The goddess, Mahadevi, is present in all female beings, "Women are goddesses, women are life itself"—*striyo devah, siriyan pranah*—is written in a Tantric text. This gives rise, first of all, to the cult of women and of virgins (*kumari*). In operative Tantrik, women often take the name of the goddess herself and are called *shakti* or *prakriti*, which in the Samkhya system is the corresponding cosmic principle. From this it is but a short step to consider woman and union with her as a means of participating in the sacrum. Indeed, in the Tantrik the part of an initiator, of a *guru*, is also attributed to woman. This should not be understood in an intellectual sense, as meaning that the woman transmits the teaching (as is the case in the branch of the Tantra known as Nigama, in which it is the Goddess who instructs the God in the doctrine). Rather it should be understood

---

Shakti and Shakta, pp. 97 ff.

[12] L. De La Vallée Poussin, *Bouddhisme, Etudes et materiaux* (Paris, 1898), p. 138. See Prapancasara Tantra, IX, pp. 23–24.

as meaning that a special sort of woman can transmit to the man a certain kind of influence whose effects may be spiritual enlightenment and awakening. The general principle of Tantra is the idea of overcoming the antithesis between liberation (*mukthi*) and enjoyment (*bhoga*), the attainment of both at one and the same time, differing in this from the ascetic forms of Yoga. This leads to rites in which both women and intoxicating beverages are used, not for the purposes which might interest the profane, carnal-minded, and "bound" man (*pashu*), but to favor ecstasy, contact, and union with the goddess, which is the principle of liberation. This is the loftiest sense of the secret ritual known as *pancatattva* of the Hindu Tantrik of the Left Hand (*vamacara*).[13] This is also the meaning of some forms of the Vajrayana in which a strange type of Buddha is presented to us, who vanquishes Mara, the god of death, and obtains enlightenment and special powers by uniting sexually with women. Agreement with the aims of the purely intellectual Yoga can be noted in such expressions as the following: "Having meditated in this way, the *sadhaka* should worship the Devi (the Goddess) as his own *atma*, thinking: I am Brahman" (Kali Tantra, IX, 16), and "A *sadhaka* should meditate on his own self as one and the same with her (the Goddess, *Shakti*) *taya sahi tam atmanam ekabhutam vicintayet*" (Kubjka Tantra, II, 3). The "power of liberating the essence of the Ego" is ascribed to the Tantric woman, to the *shaktis* or *yoginis*.[14] From more than one point of view, the effects of sex-initiation are thought of as equal to those of the awakening of the *kundalini*, of which the Hatha Yoga speaks. Indeed, in this mysterious and dangerous power, the awakening of which produces liberation even in this life (*jivanmukti*), is seen the Goddess as she is present in the human being, the "inner woman." The rite of the awakening (*bodhana*) in the traditional ceremony of the *Durga-Puja* (the cult of Durga, one of the forms of the Goddess) is also explained esoterically as a suggestion of awakening, or attaining consciousness of *kundalini*. On the other hand, the relation of *kundalini* to sex and to woman, and to the power of which

---

[13] See J. Woodroffe, *Shakti and Shakta*, cit., passim.
[14] Von Glasenapp, *Buddhistische Mysterien*, p. 56.

woman is mainly the embodiment, is shown by the fact that *kundalini* is evoked and seen in the woman by the eye of the mind in the proceedings of some popular sexual spells.[15]

Let us consider some other details of the Tantra to illustrate other points in which it is comparable to the Western forms of the "Mysteries of Woman."

In these Western forms, the woman, as has been said, was also related to Sophia, to the Gnosis, the transcendent intelligence. In India the Goddess offers these aspects also. In a hymn to the *Mahadevi* [Great Goddess] contained in the fifth *matamya* of the *Chandi*, it is said that the Goddess in each being is known as intelligence, that she resides in every being under the form of *buddhi*. In a hymn to Durga in the Visvasana Tantra, she is addressed as *buddhida*, i.e., "the dispenser of *buddhi*."[16] Now, *buddhi* is the equivalent of the transcendent intellect of which the Fedeli d'Amore spoke. The women used in the Tantric practices contain this principle potentially, if one of the names by which they are known is, in addition to *shakti* and *mudra*, also *vidya*, which means knowledge, wisdom—not in an intellectualistic and abstract sense, but as a power of enlightenment.

In the Buddhist Tantras, woman is related to *prajna*, which has the same meaning. The union of the man with the woman has here the value of an initiation; it realizes or announces the Great Liberation which, according to the Mahayana doctrine, arises from the union of *prajna* with *upaya*, these principles being contained in woman and in man.[17]

There were circles in Bengal which developed a theology, or rather a scholasticism, about love and desire in terms analogous to those of the courts of love of the West. Broadly speaking, Tantrik also knows Platonic Love. We meet with it not only in the aforesaid terms of a cult of woman as the incarnation of the De-

---

[15] See R. Schmidt, *Indische Erotik* (Berlin: Hermann Barsdorf Verlag, 1910), pp. 676–77.

[16] A. & E. Avalon, *Hymns to the Goddess* (London: Luzac & Co., 1913), pp. 128–30, 139.

[17] See S. Dasgupta, *Obscure Religious Cults*, p. xxxvii; see Chapter 5, pp. 33–37.

vi, but also in the operative field, for the rituals of the Left-Hand
Tantrik also have two phases: the phase in which the woman is
only "adored" precedes that in which she is possessed. On this
subject one text details a long and complicated procedure. The
man must live with the woman and serve her for long months,
sharing her room and even her bed, but avoiding all physical
contact, limiting himself to adoring her and fervently desiring
her. It is only after this apprenticeship of Platonic Love, which
must last not less than nine months, that sexual union is allowed
to the disciple.[18] But this union is of a special kind, for there
must be no issue of seminal fluid.[19] The feature that differenti-
ates the Tantric experiences from those which can be glimpsed
in the writings of the Fedeli d'Amore is that a form of rapture is
required, like that of Platonic Love, and cultivated in various
ways—a rapture which, however, continues in the act of physical love without losing its specific characteristics. In other words,
while in the Western forms to which we have just referred, the
final aim is a kind of occult union with the female principle on a
hyperphysical plane, the Tantrik holds that it is possible to realize and intensify this union through the possession of the woman as *yogini*, *shakti*, or *vidya*.

Another point to be noted: the ancient Hindu tradition had
already associated the principle of inebriation with the Great
Goddess. It has been observed that one of her forms is Varunani,
an entity on whom the name of Sura and also of Varuni was later bestowed. But in Pali, Varuni designates an intoxicating beverage, as well as a woman who is intoxicated. There can be no
doubt of the connection between Varuni and inebriating drinks,
indeed in some texts "to drink *devi varuni*" means to drink such

---

[18] See *An Introduction to the Study of the Post-Chaitanya Sahajiya Cult*,
pp. 77–78 (quoted by M. Eliade, *Yoga: Immortality and Freedom*, pp. 266–
7). Other details on this ritual are found in the Nayika-sadhana-Tika (=
a commentary on dealings with women). When transferred to the hyperphysical plane, the erotic union "never comes to an end" (cf. M. Eliade, p. 267).

[19] See M. Eliade, pp. 259 ff.; G. Tucci, *Tibetan Painted Scrolls* (Rome:
Libreria dello Stato, 1949), vol. I, p. 242; Evola, *The Yoga of Power*, pp.
123 ff.

beverages.[20] Even in the hymns of the austere Shankara, the Goddess is associated with inebriating beverages; she either holds the cup or is inebriated.[21] Thus, in this divine archetype is stressed the aspect of the feminine principle as a source of rapture and inebriation. This conception is also reflected in the association of the use of the woman with the use of intoxicating drinks in the secret ritual of the Left-Hand Tantrik. In one of the texts of this branch of the Tantra, wine is called the "Goddess as Savior in liquid form — *Tara dravamayi*" (Mahanirvana Tantra, XI, 105–107). Here we have a return of the idea that she is the source both of enjoyment and liberation. Thus, the reference is more or less to the sacred effects that were ascribed to inebriation by the ancient Thracian cult of Dionysus.[22]

The important thing in all this, however, is that inebriation must undergo a transformation, a change in its nature, for which the technical expression used is *aropa*. The same holds good also, and above all, for the sexual climax. These practices, therefore, are not suited to all and their dangers have been clearly recognized. Initiation is required of those who, being true Kaulas, wish to make use of intoxicants (Mahanirvana Tantra, X, 112). Certain ascetic qualities are also presupposed for the Yogic rites with the woman, with the *shakti*. That women as the bearers of the Goddess also embody the principle of rapture is made clear by yet another Tantric designation currently applied to them: *rati* = the principle of *rasa*, a word which means rapture, intense emotion, and also orgasm. In the myth, Rati is the bride of Kama, the god of love. The Sahajiya school has worked out a whole

---

[20] J. Przyluski, *La Grande Déesse* (Paris: Payot, 1950), p. 139.

[21] In Avalon, *Hymns to the Goddess*, pp. 26–28, 58–59.

[22] Mahanirvana Tantra (XI, 105–7) expresses itself in the following terms on the intoxicating drinks used by the Kaulas: "Wine is Tara herself in liquid form, who is the savior of beings, the giver of enjoyment and liberation, who destroys danger and diseases, burns up the heaps of sins. . . . O Adya! She (wine) is ever taken by those who have attained final liberation, by those who are desirous of attaining final liberation, by those that have become and those striving to be adepts." (XI, 108): "Mortals who drink wine with their mind well under control and according to the injunctions are verily immortals on earth."

scholastic classification of the type of the *ratis* which must be selected for efficient experience. The type best suited is that of the
vishesa-rati, the "exceptional woman," in whom we may recognize a parallel of the "Lady of the Miracle" of whom the Fedeli
d'Amore wrote.[23]

In the Sahajiya school we meet with the expression "death in
love," and it is said that only through that death can one "really
live."[24] This matches precisely a recurrent theme in the literature
of the Fedeli d'Amore of the West, and also in that of some Islamic Sufis (Jalal ad-Din Rumi, for instance). In this literature we
also meet with the motif of a deadly wound and of a kind of
fulmination produced by the love or by the apparition of the Lady. Likewise, in a hymn of the Tantrasara, it is said of the Goddess: "Thou dost ascend like a streak of lightening."[25] In the
Buddhist Tantra, the chief effect of sexual Yoga is the awakening
of the *bodhicitta*, i.e., of the "thought-enlightenment," like a flash
ascending from the trunk of the body towards the brain.[26] If, it is
said, the semen is arrested at the "identity of enjoyment," *manas*
is killed: "the mind dies and the breath of life is also extin-
guished" — these are the words of the *Saraha-pada*.[27] We have
here the equivalent of the ecstasy and *excessus mentis* of the
Fedeli d'Amore. When the Goddess evoked in the woman has
the dreadful and destructive aspects of Kali and Durga, it was
probably this effect of initiatic death that was considered from
an esoteric standpoint. The Western parallel is to be found in
"Diana invulnerable and deadly"; perhaps a similar experience
is referred to in Hermetism by the saying "to see Diana entirely
naked." In its positive aspect it is the realization of *sahaja* — the
"un-born," the "unconditioned" through *mahasukha*, the supreme ecstasy of bliss in which *samarasa*, the emotional fusion of
male and female in the sexual climax, is transformed.

---

[23] Dasgupta, *Obscure Religious Cults*, pp. 162–63.

[24] Ibid., p. 160.

[25] *Hymns to the Goddess*, p. 35.

[26] Dasgupta, pp. 29–30; Tucci., vol. I, p. 242.

[27] Dasgupta, p. 93; Eliade, *Yoga*, p. 268; N. Shahidullah, *Les chants
mystiques des Kanha et des Doha kosha* (Paris: Adrien-Maisonneuve,
1928).

We can stop at this point in our parallels between the Western and Oriental forms of the "Mysteries of Woman." Apart from India, the practices of Chinese Taoism also make use of sex for the purposes of initiation. But it cannot be said for certain that such practices can be classified with those of the Mysteries of Woman, as they would seem to be quite lacking in the idea of woman as the incarnation of a divinity and the dispenser of a vivifying and enlightening power. Woman embodies only the *yin* principle, just as man embodies the *yang* principle, which is that to which preeminence and a celestial character are attributed in the Far Eastern tradition. It would seem that in the Taoist rites, woman served only as a means, and some texts even advise that she should not know that in joining with her the man has initiation in mind. Other texts give reason to suspect that in some cases the purpose served is even a form of masculine vampirism.[28]

It would seem that in the West the practice of the Mysteries of Woman has been continued down to modern times. On this matter mention may be made in the first place of the work by P. B. Randolph, *Magia Sexualis* (Paris: G. Le Prat, 1952),[29] in which reference is made to the practices of an organization known as the Eulis Brotherhood, which engaged in its activities towards the close of last century. In the second place we would mention the "Law of Thelema," announced by Aleister Crowley, in which sexual rites play an important part, with intentionally blasphemous and satanic tones. This may have been only partially in keeping with the real facts, the rest being the result of Crowley's irresistible desire to *épater le bourgeois*, and defy the anger of Anglo-Saxon puritanism.[30]

East & West, vol. 9, no. 4 (1958): pp. 349–55

---

[28] The best accounts of Taoist sexual practices are found in the lengthy essay by Maspero, "Les procédés de nourrir l'esprit vital dans la religion taoïste ancienne."

[29] English edition: *Magia Sexualis: Sexual Practices for Magical Power*, trans. Donald Traxler (Rochester, Vt: Inner Traditions, 2012).—Eds.

[30] Some information can be gathered from J. Symonds, *The Great Beast: The Life of Aleister Crowley* (London: Rider, 1952).

PHILOSOPHY & RELIGION:
THE EGYPTIAN & TIBETAN
BOOKS OF THE DEAD

Boris de Rachewiltz
Il libro dei Morti degli antichi Egiziani
Milan: All'Insegna del Pesce d'Oro, 1958

This publication fills a void long felt by many students of the history of religions, since previous editions of the Book of the Dead, this most important document of ancient Egypt, have long been unavailable. The works of Lepsius (1842), Naville (1886), Pierret (1882), Sir Peter Le Page Renouf (1904), and Schiaparelli (1881–1890) can only be found in libraries. The only volume reprinted has been the 1953 edition by E. A. Wallis Budge with facsimiles of the papyri.

Mention should also be made of the G. Kolpaktchy edition published in French and Italian. But it is of little use from the scientific point of view, for the author, animated by the praiseworthy desire to give the inner esoteric sense of many passages of the text, has too often been carried away by his imagination, or, worse still, allowed himself to be influenced by dubious ideas taken from modern Theosophy.

This handsomely printed edition and translation by De Rachewiltz is based on the Turin papyrus, photographic reproductions of which face the pages of the translation so that anyone who wishes may compare the two. The text is of the Saite Book of the Dead, which is more recent than the Theban version. It was studied and reproduced only by Lepsius, and is more complete than the Theban version, as it represents the final stage of its development in which the basic themes have been preserved, apart from several re-elaborations and additions.

The translation is such that it can serve the purposes of both the specialist and the cultivated reader interested in the documents of traditional spirituality. For such readers, a little glossary has been added to the translation, which explains the leading themes of the Egyptian mythical-religious world that recur in the text. The translation adheres in the main to the literal meaning, but it does so in a way that generally does not hinder a symbolic or esoteric interpretation, which texts of this kind always allow.

It would be interesting — and would come within the scope of this review — to draw a comparison between the Egyptian Book of the Dead and the Tibetan Bardo Thödol, first made known by Evans-Wentz and later by Professor Tucci (who used a more complete text). The idea common to both is that, after death, the soul still has the ability to take actions on which its fate will depend. It can, in a certain way, overcome destiny, modifying the course it would otherwise follow. To express it in Oriental terms, it may be said that the soul has the power of suspending the effects of *karma*.

It should be noted, however, that this does not refer to just any kind of soul. The Tibetan text shows that the soul is always that of a person who had already travelled part of the way to liberation during his lifetime.

In the case of the Egyptian text, De Rachewiltz points out that it became the Book of the Dead for all only through a process of "democratization." In the ancient Empire it had been reserved exclusively to members of the Royal House and of the high priesthood. Indeed, originally the so-called "Osirification" was reserved for them only, and only to them was attributed the *ka*, the "double," destined to make way for the *sahu*, the immortal body that "stands up," that "does not fall."

The real title of the Egyptian text is The Book to Lead Out to the Day. The real meaning of this expression, imperfectly understood by several translators, alludes to the supreme purpose: to go out into the day means to go out into the immortal light, the invisible light of Amenti. In the Tibetan ritual, as is well known, the meeting with absolute light is the first experience and the first test encountered by the soul of the dead. An essential part of the Egyptian ritual is overcoming "the second death," that is to say the disintegration of the spiritual and psychic nucleus detached from the body by the first death (the death of the physical organism). In this connection the motive of an existential danger, of a fundamental risk encountered in the beyond, often acquires highly dramatic features in the Egyptian text. At the same time, the Egyptian text attributes more importance to behavior of a magic and determinative character than does the Tibetan, which accentuates rather the importance and power of knowledge.

Nevertheless, there are many parallel points between the two texts dealing with the liberating identifications. Just as in the Tibetan ritual the destruction of the appearance of distinct entities (which all things perceived in the experience of the other world may acquire) is indicated as a means of liberation, so in the Egyptian text formulas are repeated by means of which the soul of the dead affirms and realizes its identity with the divine figures.

In addition to these, there are the formulas for "transformation." The soul acquires the capacity of making itself manifest in the form of one or other of the cosmic powers, which in the text are made to correspond mostly to the symbolic theriomorphic figures. It is only through a misinterpretation of these references that some have been led to suppose that the doctrine of reincarnation was part of the ancient esoteric teachings of the Egyptians.

Unfortunately, the Egyptian text as it has come down to us is not systematic in character. The formulas are often presented haphazardly. Apart from spurious features of a folkloric character, the positions taken frequently fluctuate. There are spiritual ups and downs, inner shortcomings, and invocations of a religious and mystical nature.

Yet in spite of all this, the prevailing character of the most ancient, clear, and essential portions of the text is most certainly inspired by magic. The soul humbles itself so little in the presence of the ultramundane divinities that it sometimes threatens them with destruction. This is the case even with Osiris and Ra, with reference to the principle of a kind of "transcendent virility." The soul even asserts a substantial metaphysical connection between itself and the divine essences, sometimes even declaring that its salvation is also theirs. The "opening of the mouth" (by which is meant the reacquisition of the magic power of the word, which can render the formulas efficient and irresistible), "breathing the breath of life," thus becoming a Living Being, having power over the Waters, taking a Name which does not die, these are the most luminous themes in the vicissitudes of the other world.

The Egyptian text was recited at funerals, just as the Tibetan Bardo Thödol was read to the dying and even after their death. In either case the purpose was to help the soul not to forget, to stand up and remain active. De Rachewiltz, moreover, rightly calls attention to the fact that several passages suggest that the Egyptian formulas were used also during life and were held to be useful to the living, so one may recognize in the text the character of a magic ritual in the proper meaning of the term. This may indeed apply not only to some special formulas but to the text as a whole, if it is viewed in reference to the rites of initiation. For it was unanimously believed in the ancient world that the experiences of initiation corresponded to those of life beyond the grave, and that therefore the proceedings required in either case to overcome the "second death" and reach "Osirification" were the same.

In calling attention to this new publication, we would again point out that it also constitutes an important contribution for those who wish to make a comparative study of Oriental and Western traditions which, in a certain sense, find a connecting link in the traditions of ancient Egypt.

East & West, vol. 10, nos. 1–2 (March–June 1959): pp. 126–27

ON THE PROBLEM OF THE
MEETING OF RELIGIONS
IN EAST & WEST

As *East & West* is a journal devoted not only to the study of Orientalism but also to the problem of the relations between East and West, it may not be out of place to deal here with the ideas on this subject championed for some time by Jacques Albert Cuttat, though in rather narrow circles.

Cuttat is a Swiss scholar who has devoted himself especially to the comparative study of the different spiritual and religious forms, and who in a first phase had joined the French "Traditionalist" group headed by René Guénon. Under the pseudonym Jean Thamar, he published several articles in *Études traditionnelles*, the journal published by Guénon's group, as well as others under his own name in *Thought* and in *Études Asiatiques*, where his essay on the *Prajnaparamita* had also appeared. Considered from the academic standpoint, Cuttat has taught at the École pratique des Hautes Études in Paris, and is now visiting Professor at Columbia University in New York. Before that he had studied the *hexychasm*, i.e., the mysticism of the Greco-Orthodox orientation, and Arab Sufism in their homelands. It may be that it was only during this period that a strange regressive change occurred in the direction of his thought, which has led him to the ideas he now professes on the relations between Oriental and Western spirituality.

The essence of these ideas is set forth in his book *La rencontre des religions* [*The Meeting of Religions*], published in Paris in 1957 by Aubier (Éditions Montaigne), of which there is an Italian translation (Naples: Rocco, 1958).[1] Some essays and lectures of

---

[1] English edition: *The Encounter of Religions: A Dialogue Between the West and the Orient, with an Essay on the Prayer of Jesus*, trans. Pierre de Fontnouvelle and Evis McGrew (New York: Desclée, 1960). — Eds.

his may also be mentioned, among which are "Asiens Incognito im europäischen Geistesleben" [Asia Incognito in European
Spiritual Life] delivered at the University of Frankfurt, and
"Vergeistigungstechnik und Umgestaltung in Christus" [Spir-
itualization Techniques and Transformation in Christianity].
These are the writings to which we shall specifically refer to
herein.

Cuttat's new direction is parochially Christian, along lines
reminiscent of those followed by Henri Massis in his well-
known book *Défense de l'Occident*.[2] It is a kind of reaction
against the growing interest in Oriental doctrines in the West.
The arguments brought forward by Massis were extremely
primitive, and their inconsistency and partiality could be seen
at a glance. Cuttat is much better prepared. The experience he
had previously acquired enables him to put together a much
more thorough knowledge of Oriental traditions and of the
field of the comparative study of religions in general. But he
uses this superior equipment in support of an agenda like that
advanced by Massis, i.e., to denounce the "Eastern danger," to
defend the exclusivism of devotional religion of the theistic
type, and to try to assure the preeminence of this religion over
any other form of spirituality.

The purpose is therefore just the opposite of what the title *La
Rencontre des religions* might suggest. The contribution made by
Cuttat consists rather, as we shall see, in accentuating the irrec-
oncilable character, the impossibility for different spiritual
points of view of finding a meeting point.

We purposely use the expression "spiritual points of view"
instead of "religions." Indeed, as will at once be clearly seen,
Cuttat's worst misunderstandings arise from arbitrarily including under the single category of "religion" spiritual tendencies
that are not at all on the same level. And we have the right to
ask ourselves whether on this point Cuttat is not in bad faith,
that is to say whether, for the purposes of the case he pleads, he

---

[2] *Defense de l'Occident* (Paris: Plon, 1927); English edition: *Defence of
the West*, trans. by F. S. Flint (New York: Harcourt, Brace & Co, 1928),
with a Preface by G. K. Chesterton. — Eds.

acts as though he did not know the very thing which in his previous experience he had known very well: the essential morphological differences existing between religious thought and metaphysical thought, between esoterism and exoterism, between "metaphysics" and simple faith. These categories are confused and deformed by Cuttat for the purpose of exalting the originality and superiority of the religion that has come to prevail in the West, considered in its more limited and external aspects. This is very bad, and is one of the reasons that have led us to write these present notes. Even if, as we have remarked, the range of action of Cuttat's ideas is a rather modest one, there will certainly be many who will be tempted to make use of them for purposes differing widely from those of a truly objective clarification.

In examining the relations between East and West, Cuttat sets forth a series of antitheses, some of which are real, but which should merely be the object of morphological-existential considerations, exclusive of any judgment of their value, for, as has been said, the terms dealt with cannot be placed on the same plane.

Here is the way in which the problem is faced: On the one hand, there is a "spiritual hemisphere" including Jews, Christians, and Muslims, which conceives of the Absolute as a person; opposite to it there is another spiritual hemisphere, inclusive of Buddhism, Hinduism, Taoism, Confucianism, and Shintoism, for which the Absolute in its ultimate and transcendent divine reality is impersonal, and is personal only in its relative aspects and in its immanent manifestation.

Cuttat's more sophisticated approach is made manifest by the fact that he does not characterize Western spirituality as mere monotheism, and he does not use, as many do, the disparaging qualification of "pantheism" (= everything is God) for the East; he admits that "the East is perfectly aware of the divine transcendency, and in no way deifies nature as such. A much better world would be Panentheism ('everything is in God') which, instead of culminating in the Personal God, like Monotheism, ends in what Rudolf Otto calls 'Theopantism'

('God is everything,' He is the only Reality)."[3] Still more precise
is this assertion, corresponding to pure truth: "This is not to say
that the non-Christian forms of asceticism are ignorant of the
divine Transcendency and Personality, as some have claimed.
Nevertheless, they consider the second as a 'nonsupreme' facet
of the first, an aspect which will eventually fade away, when
knowledge rises to the original Non-Duality."[4]

But in this case, it is no longer a question of the presence or
non-presence of the conception of God as a person, but of the
rank assigned to this conception in a given system. And the
alternative is between systems which admit a non-personal or
super-personal Absolute, and systems which are ignorant of,
exclude, or deny this truly transcendent dimension of the Divine. But to state the question in these terms means to solve it,
in a sense, in all respects opposite to the approach taken by
Cuttat.

Before explaining why this is the case, it is to be noted that
Cuttat can refer to the antithesis between these two different
systems of East and West only in as much as he considers as
unessential, foreign, and distorting a number of doctrines that
are present alike in the traditions he includes "in the non-
Oriental spiritual hemisphere": Jewish, Christian, Islamic. (We
will not stop here to discuss the legitimacy of considering as
non-Oriental the Hebraic and Islamic traditions.) Judaism has
indeed known the Kabbalah; Islam, Sufism; and in the case of
the traditions of antiquity, Pythagoreanism, Neo-Platonism,
and many traditions of the Mysteries have been characterized
as well by the recognition of that dimension of the Absolute
that transcends the personal, theistic God. In Christianity itself,
both in its origins (especially in Dionysius the Areopagite, Ire-
neus, Synesius, and many others) and in the great mystics or
theologians that we might say are of the "dry path" (such as
Scotus Eriugena, Meister Eckhart, Tauler, etc.), we find here
and there references to this superior metaphysical dimension.

As Cuttat cannot be ignorant of all this, he has recourse to a

---

[3] Cuttat, *The Encounter of Religions*, p. 32. — Eds.
[4] Ibid., pp. 105-106. — Eds.

strange expedient: in a sort of *Machtspruch* (decree), he declares that it is here a case of the intrusion or interference of a current foreign to a Western spirituality, and he begins to speak of an "Asia incognito" which, with a zeal worthy of the Holy Office, he undertakes to unmask and to denounce, not only in the doctrines of the mystics of whom we have spoken, but even in a whole series of Western philosophers, down to Kant, Schopenhauer, Hegel, and the existentialists, so as to isolate that which in his opinion is purely "Western," but which in these terms, as we shall see, is reduced to something quite unimportant, one-sided, and conditioned.

However, the fact is that here it is absolutely nonsensical to apply the geographical-cultural categories of "East" and "West." It is not a question of the intrusion of a foreign type of spirituality into a given system, but of an esoterism which in the West also has asserted itself beyond the limits of exoterism (i.e., of the more external aspects of the corresponding tradition); of a gnosis and of "metaphysics" that has gone beyond the realm of mere faith. Therefore, as has been pointed out, it is not even a question of a "religion" that meets, or does not meet, with another religion on the same plane, but of spiritual categories or worlds that are quite different. To be more precise, it is a question of the morphological difference existing between systems that, in addition to "religion," have metaphysical teachings, and systems that instead begin and end on the plane of devotional religion. Cuttat has done his best to restrict the *whole* "Western" tradition to a system of the second type, which is as arbitrary as it is one-sided.

In any case, as he has been compelled to recognize the existence of an Eastern system of metaphysics, he finds himself in a position impossible to defend when he tries to present the matter in a light advantageous to theism. It would be consistent to assert that it is impossible to conceive an impersonal Absolute beyond the personal one, by declaring that all doctrines based on such a conception are delusions and aberrations. But unless this is done, if one admits as conceivable a superpersonal and impersonal God beyond the theistic God, a principle anterior and superior to the Divinity conceived in the image of the human figure, then it is absolutely absurd to claim for the latter preeminence over the former.

Cuttat is thus forced to have recourse to a mere verbal device to give an appearance of consistency to his attempt to invert the aspects. As a matter of fact, when he does not follow in the footsteps of those who would settle all questions about non-Christian spirituality by describing it as "naturalistic" or "pantheistic" mysticism; when instead of so doing he speaks, with reference to the "East," of an "impersonal divinity who is, indeed, ontological or metaphysical but not supernatural" (the theistic divinity would instead be supernatural), he twists the meaning of the words, because the literal meaning of the expression "metaphysical" (*physis* = nature) is "supernatural," "metacosmic." And as Cuttat has had to admit that the East is acquainted with a metacosmic principle, he invents a new and non-sensical expression, "transmetacosmic," in the opinion that this cheap verbal expedient will suffice to afford a basis for his supremacist pleading.

Cuttat believes that in connection with the "transmetacosmic" principle, man could inaugurate relations of a superior nature, not ontological but personal and "truly spiritual," unknown to the "East." Here again he displays uncommon skill in shuffling the cards on the table, as he gives the impression of having taken into consideration all that refers to "Eastern" spirituality, but he does so only to assign it an inferior and subordinate position. And here we enter into the field of the experiences of the inner life. To characterize the "Eastern" path, some have spoken not of ecstasy but of "enstasy": that is to say of a concentric movement, of detachment of the mind from the object and from the external world of phenomena; of an interiorizing convergence towards the deeper Ego, the divine Self.

Cuttat hastens to make use of this idea. This, for him, would be "the primal gesture of the East." But only half of the distance would thus have been traversed. Having reached his own center, man would have to recognize the "vertical transcendence," and a movement would have to be made toward the personal God who is "unattainable transcendence" standing above all interiority, even the deepest and the most detached from the world. And here the only categories that would count would be the "moral" Christian ones, or those of a Christian type, no longer the "ontological" Eastern ones. The category of the relation between an "I" and a "Thou," of the human person with the Divine Person, love or supernatural *communio*, confidence in the redemption enacted by Christ (thus automatically Hebraism and Islamism would fall out of the "non-Eastern spiritual hemisphere"), faith, humility, the "tremendous amazement" as the reply of man to God "who wishes to give Himself to him," and who has placed it in the creature in order to reveal Himself to him as the being above him, and so forth.

The conclusion at which he arrives with admirable ease is that, "the East has not yet explicitly discovered that the extreme interiority of the Spirit culminates in the extreme transcendency of the Creator."[5] In other words, the whole East is reduced to nothing but a mere preparatory stage, a possible *via purgationis*, beyond which only the truly supernatural reveals itself.

All this makes apparent the intention to create confusion, *pour cause*. Cuttat acts as though he did not know what he does indeed know, for, if not directly from the traditions themselves, he has learned the real structure of the path in "metaphysical" doctrines at least from the clear statement of their real meaning made by the "Traditionalist" group. Those doctrines take into consideration both directions, which are related to the symbolism of the center (or pole) and to that of the axis. The first movement is just that toward the interior (enstasy) by which the deepest and most original nucleus of one's own being is reached, detached from all "nature." The Ego itself as center is, however, far from being the point of arrival; it is, in its turn, the starting point for the "vertical" realization of the transcendent and super-individual states of being along "the Axis of the World," symbolized in various ways by the different traditions, and leading to the unconditioned.

All this had been clearly seen by the metaphysical teachings—it is, in a way, related by the Ancients to the distinction

---

[5] Ibid., p. 32. — Eds.

between the Lesser Mysteries and the Greater Mysteries, and in
the Far East to the distinction between "real man" and "transcendent man." Therefore, the distinctive feature of the view
upheld by Cuttat and attributed to "Western" spirituality consists solely in conceiving of a *split* between the two phases: the
line of a true *realization* stops at the center; the being does not
rise above the center following the vertical direction. As though
brought to a standstill by impotence or by fundamental anguish, he (the being) objectivizes all the other states in the form
of a transcendent person, the unattainable theistic God, retreating from the plane of metaphysical and intellectual realization
to that of emotion, love, faith, and all the rest, giving new life to
all those purely human motives, at bottom conditioned, social-
ly and affectively. Cuttat refers indeed to relations similar to
those between friend and friend, between bridegroom and
bride, between father and son—which the preliminary process
of "catharsis" and "enstasis" should have burnt without leaving any remainder. Undoubtedly, metaphysics also recognizes
that between the concentric and the vertical realization there is
a rupture of continuity, a hiatus; but it is just the ability to sur-
mount this hiatus actively that gives to the real initiate his
chrism. This is the essential point.

Here also the concessions Cuttat had to make as regards the
"Oriental" metaphysical path irremediably injure from the start
the ideas for which he stands, the cause of the "West." He admits that that path is characterized by depersonalization, by the
overcoming of the personality and attainment of a naked Ego,
which, like the *nous*, is pre-conceptual, pre-affective, pre-
volitional. How then can it be possible to refer to a higher
stage, a type of relationship in which everything that is not only "personal" but even sentimental, emotional, and "moral"
plays the decisive part? Do not the relations of love, even if it is
mystic love, in themselves imply the limit of personality?
Moreover, how can one seriously bring a charge of "subjectivi-
ty" and of "individualism" against a mind which has attained,
through an intellectual catharsis, that form of depersonalized
nakedness of which we have spoken?

We have said that the "Oriental" path was not unaware of

"vertical transcendence," but conceived it as the task of realization. To make apparent all the absurdity of considering as a higher degree that which arises not from realization but from an arrest of the being at *the beginning* of the vertical direction, with the consequent return of sub-intellectual complexes, let us just try to imagine a Yogi or a Siddha who begins to weep (in theistic mysticism the "gift of tears" is given as one of the highest marks of perfection in the Saint), a Buddha who starts praying and invoking, a Taoistic *shen-jen* or "transcendent man," or a master of Zen who repeats formulae of the type of the *hesychasm*: "Jesus Christ, Son of God, have mercy on me!" and such like. The impossibility of conceiving anything of the kind shows, better than any dialectics, the absurdity of the views of Cuttat and the level to which they belong.

The only merit our Author can claim is that of having made a thorough examination of the implications of a purely religious position alien to all forms of metaphysics. He thus ends by denying even the value of that movement of "concentric" or enstatic realization of the Ego that he had accepted as the first phase of the process as a whole. He sees the danger of the idea that "God unites only with gods" (it is a saying of St. Simeon, but it is also a classical and Pythagorean notion); preliminary *theosis* (divinization) is, at bottom, superfluous and dangerous, for "we are already redeemed in Christ" (here again Islamism and Hebraism fall away), and all that need be done is to adhere humbly and believingly in our Redeemer. Cuttat writes:

> And, above all, are we not forcing upon God more than He asks of us, when we refuse to ascend toward Him from the starting point of our fallen nature? Is it not precisely for that nature, for the sick, the outcast, the sinners, and even the dead, that Christ expressly intended His act of Redemption? Has He placed on His greatest promises any *sine qua non* condition other than that of unreservedly surrendering ourselves, as we are, as He finds us, with our shortcomings, to the Almightiness of His essentially gratuitous and undeserved Mercy? To believe that we may approach Him and unite ourselves to Him only after

having bathed all our wounds is to lay down our own stipulations for this required surrender, to deny Him our absolute confidence, to doubt that He alone is the author of our deifying redemption, and to deem it impossible (because insufficient) that the only co-operation expected of us be precisely this confident but unconditional surrender.[6]

This means the renunciation even of the attempt to include, be it only as a preparatory and subordinate phase, what had been formerly recognized as valid, in the "Oriental" ascetic and realizing line (reduced to very little indeed), and leads more or less to the Calvinistic doctrine — the extreme limit of the purely religious direction — that rejects works and sees in faith alone the instrument of possible salvation.

And here again Cuttat, to avoid having to pass over in silence facts with which he is well acquainted but which would destroy his theories, tries to shuffle the cards. The East indeed has also known a type of man who can accept the aforesaid views: he is the Bhakta, the devotional type, and the East also has known a similar path, the *Bhaktimarga*, which possesses more or less the same categories mentioned above, with a personal divinity as the supreme term of reference. Two points should be noted, however: the first is that in India the Bhakta is considered as a type of man who, being characterized by the so-called *rajas*-quality, ranks below the type who follows the path of pure metaphysical knowledge, characterized by the superior *sattva*-quality (it is a question of the doctrine of the three *gunas*). In the second place the appearance of the Bhaktic current, whether in India or elsewhere, is historically a relatively late event; more precisely, it is only recently that it has acquired importance and come to the fore other than as a trend of the more popular and promiscuous forms of worship. In order to face this fact Cuttat again shuffles the cards, helping himself now with the Western conception of time.

He speaks of the opposition that exists in regard to time be-

---

[6] Ibid., p. 128. — Eds.

tween the Judeo-Christian view of creation from which, in his opinion, proceeds the idea of historical development, more or less in terms of progress, and the "Eastern" conception of the world as an unchangeable emanation, as a pure symbol and perpetual image of a metacosmic and timeless reality, a conception which excludes the idea of historical development, and gives rise to the doctrine of cycles: time that consumes itself in a recurrent circular process which has no meaning in itself, but only as "the moving image of eternity." We will not make note of the fact that the second conception, if it is not that proper to Christianity (though it appears in Ecclesiastes), was however familiar to many doctrines of Western and Mediterranean antiquity. Were we to do so, Cuttat would hasten to say that it is a case of an "intrusion of Asia" or of an "Asia *incognito*." Nor will we go back to what Celsus ironically pointed out in this connection, when he said that it is because they know only a fragment of a cycle that the Christians and the Jews speak so much of "history" and of "the end of the world," dramatizing the one and the other, mistaking a recurrent episode for the whole. However this may be, the conflict between the "evolutionary" conception (even if with a providential or eschatological background) and the involutionary conception of history is real, and apart from the timeless metaphysical openings of history, it corresponds — if we study the ages known to us — to the conflict between an illusion and the truth, a truth that is becoming more and more apparent in the West.

Now, taking in hand the historical-evolutionary conception, Cuttat thinks he has found the means of getting over in an elegant way the difficulty caused by the aforesaid late character of the *bhakti* theory in the East, by stating that it is precisely here that we should see the progress proper to a superior stage of evolution. In his opinion we have here something that enters into the plan of a "divine economy" which has bestowed even on the East, at a later stage, a truth and a path similar to that revealed by Christianity, the God of the *bhakti-marga* being a hidden, not yet recognized form of the very God of the "monotheistic revelation."

But the fact is that the late appearance of the devotional doctrine in the East is part of a regressive process (it falls in fact exactly within the period known as the "dark age," Kali Yuga); it is due to the "covering up" of doctrines that were originally metaphysical, and to the popularization of those doctrines. This can be clearly seen in the case both of Buddhism and Taoism. Only when they both became popular, when they were opened more and more to the masses, only then did the constant features of all that is mere religion take shape: reliance on the gods to obtain salvation, the transformation into "Divine Persons" of abstract metaphysical principles or of great spiritual teachers, the need of external spiritual help, faith, devoutness, worship, and collective ceremonies. Only if it is "providential" to create illusions and to compromise with human weaknesses, only then can the processes that in several Oriental traditions have led regressively to such results — the most typical case is that of Amidism — be considered as "providential." This is one episode of that general involutionary trend of mankind — first in the West, and then also in the East — which today only those who shut their eyes so as not to see could fail to discern, for it is becoming every day more apparent. The fact of the chronological syntony of Western devoutness with the spread of Bhaktism, Amidism, religious Taoism, etc., this coincidence may have escaped — as Cuttat says it has — the attention both of Orientalists and of Western missionaries, and of the Oriental who takes an interest in Western Christianity; but it is nevertheless obvious, and its real meaning is strictly that which we have indicated.

Were we to call attention to all the manipulations to which Cuttat has had recourse, we should never come to an end. We will not therefore stop to note how he treats Islam, here again inverting the facts; for it is precisely Islam with Sufism (which goes so far as to recognize in man the condition in which the Absolute becomes aware of itself, and which professes the doctrine of the Supreme Identity) that affords a clear and eloquent example of a system which, though it includes a strictly theistic religious domain, recognizes a loftier truth and path of realization. The emotional and devotional elements, love and all the rest, lose here — as is the case with the authentic Buddhism of the origins—all "moral" significance, and all intrinsic value, and acquire the significance only of one of the many techniques (as is indeed the case with Bhaktism itself, if rightly understood).

In conclusion, the contribution made by Cuttat consists, as has been said, in defining strictly and consistently that which belongs to a purely exclusivist religious doctrine, as opposed to a metaphysical doctrine. The antitheses to which he calls attention are indeed real ones from the point of view of the former: on the one hand, moral—i.e., non-real—categories, on the other hand, ontological categories; on the one hand, the ideal of deification or sacralization, on the other, the ideal of simple sanctification; on the one hand, the theme of sin and guilt, on the other, the theme of the error and the theory of metaphysical ignorance; on the one hand, redemption or salvation, on the other, liberation and spiritual awakening; on the one side, objective techniques, on the other, the "response" of the soul that surrenders itself to the personal God; on the one hand, the theory of the Incarnation as a unique and unrenewable fact which divides in two halves the spiritual history of the world, on the other, the theory of the *avatara* and of multifarious divine manifestations; on the one hand, the world viewed as a sacred and transparent symbol of the timeless metacosmos, on the other, the recognition of the object and the fraternal and loving *communio* of all beings and creatures in God (as in the nature mysticism of St. Francis); on the one hand, the deconditioning of personality, on the other, the acceptance of the irremediable finitude of man as a creature; on the one hand, catharsis beyond history, on the other, the eschatological valuation of history (which on the profane level leads to Western fantasies about progress).

All these antitheses are real, or rather, as a rule, they present themselves as such if one assumes the religious standpoint characterized by conferring an absolute value on something that is proper to a lower human type, and on the "truths" suited to it. Instead, from the metaphysical standpoint, it is a question of two planes to be seen in an order of rank.

The facts, therefore, are the opposite of how Cuttat has endeavored to present them when he says that "the Western

Christian values include and complete the Eastern ones, and not vice versa." How, starting from his strange ideas and from so many misunderstandings, it is possible to suppose that the "new Euro-Asian Renaissance" and the corresponding "irresistible interpenetration between East and West" can lead to something positive, and how it is possible to speak of "meetings," in which "the East should not be used by the West to reject, perhaps unawares, its own value, but rather to stimulate it (the West) to acquire a deeper knowledge of that value" — this is what we cannot comprehend unless we are to understand "deeper" to mean the strengthening of what is presumed to be "Western" (and we have already pointed out the arbitrary nature of this identification), all that is exclusive, limited, and even anomalous.

This negative conclusion is explicitly contained in the pages in which Cuttat takes his stand towards "Traditionalism," that is to say the very current to which he himself had subscribed previously. "Traditionalism" asserts the idea of the transcendent unity of all religions, or rather of all the great spiritual traditions (for we insist in stressing the advisability of limiting the notion of "religion" to certain special forms of those traditions). From the "Traditionalist" point of view, these present themselves as homologous; as various, more or less complete forms of a unique knowledge, of a *philosophia perennis* emanating from a primordial, timeless tradition. All differences would relate to the contingent, conditioned, and caducous side, and not to the essential side of each single historical tradition, and none of these could claim to represent exclusively the absolute truth.

Now, Cuttat says, "Of all the religions, Christianity is the only one which is either the *whole Truth* or a crazy pretention. *Tertium non datur*" (here once more Cuttat has dropped, by the way, Greek thought, Islam, and all else he had included in the spiritual, "non-Oriental" hemisphere of our planet to swell its size). A Christianity which could be "homologized" would be but one religion among many; it would disperse like a mere chimaera. It is either the "incomparable" or it is nothing. In Cuttat's opinion the universal concordance, the comparability, the transcendent equivalence of religions, all that "is not a religious constant, but only an aspect of the *nonmonotheistic traditions*,"[7] for the "Western" believer to admit that his tradition may be considered from such a point of view, thus becoming "equivalent to the others before God," would mean that he abjures his faith. He adds that from the Hebraic-Christian point of view, the only possible position before other spiritual currents is not that of "homologation" but of the "conversion" of those who hold them. This amounts to putting an end, once and for all, to the formula of "meetings" and to render impossible any serious dialogue between "East and West."

Even these brief notes will have made evident the doctrinal inconsistency of the ideas of Cuttat. From the subjective standpoint, and within the framework of the spiritual movement of the times, his exclusivism is but a regressive phenomenon. It can be explained as a kind of "anguish complex." It is a desperate reassertion of definite existential limitations before the prospect of widening horizons, of a higher liberty, a liberty which, by a certain quite unmodern type of man, can only regard as destructive. For our part, we absolutely refuse to identify this type of man with that of the true man of the West.

East & West, vol. 10, no. 4 (December 1959): pp. 169–75

---

[7] Ibid., p. 77. — Eds.

VEDANTA, MEISTER ECKHART, SCHELLING

In the previous chapter we thought it opportune to criticize the manner in which, from the factious defense of a one-sidedly theistic-Christian point of view, a modern author, J. A. Cuttat, confronted the problem of the relation between Western and Eastern spirituality. We are therefore all the more pleased to now point out a recent contribution of an entirely different, more positive order, devoted to the same problem by another scholar of religious history, Walter Heinrich. It is a work first issued in three small volumes in the collection *Fragen der Zeit (Problems of Time)* by the Stifter Bibliothek (Salzburg-Klosterneuburg) and then united into a single volume by the same publisher, with the title *Verklärung und Erlösung im Vedanta, Meister Eckhart und Schelling (Transfiguration and Salvation in Vedanta, Meister Eckhart, and Schelling).*[1] Already the title indicates that it considers the latest problems of the spirit in an examination of three metaphysical systems particularly representative for East and West.

In an earlier volume of the same collection, *Über die traditionelle Methode (On the Traditional Method),*[2] Professor Heinrich had already defined the method that he follows in these studies. It is a comparative method in a special, organic sense. For Heinrich, the problem is not one of an exterior comparison between detached parts, starting from which one arrives at a whole set of correspondences of ideas or of symbols. On the contrary, it is a question of starting from the essential intuition of a content which ideally precedes the parts, and comparative research must serve to illustrate this content with the contribution given by its various forms of expression, as they present themselves to us in diverse formulations and in diverse tradi-

---

[1] *Verklärung und Erlösung im Vedanta, Meister Eckhart und Schelling* (Salzburg-Klosterneuburg: Stifterbibliothek, 1956).—Eds.

[2] *Über die traditionelle Methode* (Salzburg-Klosterneuburg: Stifterbibliothek, 1954).—Eds.

tions. In the application of this method made in the new work, Heinrich also emphasizes that the perceived concordances of the essential ideas can he explained neither by transmission nor by exterior, empirical contacts: they have a profound root of a metaphysical character. Aside from this epistemological premise, one may say that Heinrich follows in no less a measure the method of "phenomenology": he wants the evidence to speak for itself, and tries to add nothing extraneous and personal. Thus, a very large part of the book is composed of direct quotations from well-chosen texts that take their own place in the over-all picture.

It is quite evident that Heinrich takes the principal points of reference of this overall picture from the Hindu tradition, as that which has presented in the most complete and elaborate form the same contents that can be found in Eckhart and Schelling, but in a less systematic and less conscious form and also on spiritual levels that are, as we shall see, quite different. We have spoken of the Hindu tradition in general because, in reality, it is not a question of Vedanta in the narrow sense, referring only to the systems of Shankara, Ramanuja, Vallabha, or other thinkers who diverge a good deal from the pure metaphysical and intellectual line of the major Upanishads. Rather the concern here is with what has been presented as Vedanta in terms of a synthesis of pure Hindu orthodoxy by René Guénon in his work *L'homme et son devenir selon le Vedanta*.[3] And Heinrich essentially follows the "Traditional" interpretation on the high level of Guénon, who based himself less on the works of the Orientalists than on direct contacts with qualified representatives of the Hindu tradition. Heinrich, like Guénon, therefore has the merit of excluding from his exposition every naturalistic and mythological element: in myth, as well as in that which would seem to refer to phenomena and elements of nature, the internal content or pure intellectual, i.e., noetic character, is put into relief.

There is above all a meeting of Vedanta, Meister Eckhart,

---

[3] *Man and His Becoming According to the Vedanta* (Ghent, NY: Sophia Perennis, 2004).

and Schelling in that which concerns the fundamental metaphysical conception of the Supreme Unity, the Eternal One.
Everything which is manifested in the finite world is but a
"limitated" determination of a principle which is unique and of
a power which embraces every possibility. However, it is very
important to point out that it is illegitimate to apply to this doctrine the stale formula of "pantheism." It concerns rather a synthesis between transcendence and immanence that is to be referred to a super-rational plane. As a matter of fact, in all three
cases it is affirmed in the clearest terms that the principle which
is all, single, and supreme, at the same time absolutely transcends all. This doctrinal conception is confirmed by the very
nature of the highest ideal of knowledge and liberation offered
to man, an ideal which is of absolute transcendence. In particular, and as a consequence of this, the three systems agree in rejecting theism as the supreme point of reference. Beyond Ish-
vara and Brahma as creator god, beyond Saguna-Brahman for
Vedanta, there is Brahman, neuter, impersonal and superpersonal, and that which metaphysically corresponds to the so-
called "fourth state," to the *turiya*. In Eckhart it is the distinction between *Gott* (the personal God) and *Gottheit* (divinity,
neuter, impersonal) which is superior to being and is ineffable,
naked simplicity. As to Schelling, Heinrich would perhaps
have done better to have given greater importance to the ideas
of his later philosophy (the doctrine of the divine potencies)
where the Absolute is conceived as the opposite of Being, as
the non-being that realizes itself by detaching itself from its
"nature" and affirming itself as pure power.

A second consequence of the doctrine of identity, common
to all three examples, is the rejection of the conception of man
as a "creature" separated by an unbridgeable ontological
chasm from his Creator. To the Hindu doctrine of the Atman as
the metaphysical ground of the Ego, identical with Brahman,
corresponds Eckhart's conception of the *Funklein*, "not touched
either by space or by time," the idea that the soul exists eternally in God and as God, as well as his bold affirmation that "if I
did not exist, not even God would exist." Schelling speaks of
the "intellectual intuition" —*intellektuelle Anschauung*—as the

act through which one "perceives the pure absolute eternity in us, which may be said to be nothing else but the self-perception of the Absolute in us."

It is evident that by this metaphysical foundation, the religious doctrine of grace is surpassed, and the way of liberation presents itself as the way of knowledge, maintaining itself pure from every emotional, sentimental, and devotional element. Schelling and Eckhart agree with Vedanta in recognizing that the root of the human condition as such, and of every finite being in general, is "ignorance" (*avidya*). Schelling tries to explain even the religious concept of sin as ignorance. Eckhart, in a famous passage, affirms that even a stone is God, only it does not know it, and only this not-knowing determines it as what it is. Naturally, the Christian background of Eckhart does not always permit him to express himself in a rigorous way. However, the overcoming of religious conception is very clear in his doctrine of detachment, of *Abgeschiedenheit*, of *separatio*, which is developed to the point of saying that the "noble soul" must detach itself not only from exterior and material things, and in general from everything which is form and image, but also from spiritual things and from God himself—if it is to become aware of its more profound nature, that is, of that which is not natural in it, and proceed not toward God (*Gott*) but into the "desert" of the divinity (*Gottheit*), where it is alone with itself in an eternal transformation. Schelling also speaks of the point at which "it is necessary to abandon God."

The principle of detachment, of interiorization, of that which, as opposed to ecstasy, has been felicitously called "enstasy," is another common trait of the three (Eckhart: "I say that no one can know God if first he does not know himself"). But here one must recognize that the concordance regards only the general orientation. Especially in Schelling one may only speak of a postulate, of a theoretical formulation. In Eckhart an effectively lived experience may have played a part: but this experience cannot be compared with all that which Hindu tradition presents as techniques of asceticism, of high contemplation, and of Yoga.

It is because of this that the concordances that Heinrich tries to establish appear rather incomplete when it is a question of the doctrine of the deep layers of being, of the *Tiefenschichten-lehre*: they are the strata—and the states—which extend beyond the normal awakened consciousness of man and by which he is ontologically connected with the powers of reality, down to the utter root, down to the point of Supreme Identity. In Eckhart and in Schelling, only vague hints are to be found on this matter, whereas Hindu tradition knows a well-articulated and tested doctrine, with a tradition of millennia.

Heinrich emphasizes the similarities existing between eschatology, the doctrines on the *post mortem* state, and the doctrine of the metaphysical realization of the Self. As content, there is an identity between the states that eschatology, in more or less mythical form, considers for the "end of time" and for all of humanity, the states into which the soul would pass after death, and finally, the exceptional states that may be reached by those who follow the way of liberation.

As far as the first two formulations are concerned, that is, eschatology and the doctrine of the *post mortem* state, as is well known, Hindu doctrine speaks of the survival of the soul, to which first is presented the alternative between the "way of the fathers," *pitryana,* as a negative solution to which is associated the myth of reincarnation, and the "way of the gods," *devayana,* which involves the existence of a prolongation of the personality in the luminous state of *Hiranyagarbha,* or *Brahma-loka.* A further alternative is that of passing directly beyond that stage in such a way as to achieve absolute liberation, a deconditioning without residue, or in an overcoming that is, so to speak, passive, in the moment of that general crisis of manifestation to which the cosmological concept of *pralaya* is attributed. Heinrich finds elements of the same conception in Eckhart and Schelling. In Eckhart one must interpret in an adequate way that which is conceived as Purgatory and as Last Judgment. From a metaphysical point of view and not a religious one, one may see in Purgatory the intermediate state which necessarily includes the "celestial" states (distinct from the ultimate and absolute state): in the Last Judgment, the decision relative to the two alternatives of which we have just spoken. The *Brah-*

maloka as the intermediate state of a partial liberation (where he who has followed only the way of the religious cults stops) finds its correspondence in that which Schelling has called the *Geisterwelt*, the "world of spirits." Again in Schelling, the concept of "essentification" is interesting—*Essentifikation, reductio ad essentiam*: death is merely a crisis which has as its effect the destruction of the exterior and accessory and the "essentification" (the "reduction to essence") of that which man had been in life, often only uncertainly, without having had a clear knowledge of it, without maintaining himself and being faithful to himself. Here too, one has an alternative and a "judgment," because essentification extends itself to both the positive and negative qualities. Evil (that is, "ignorance," the wish of the finite, the identification with the finite) which is essentified in the *post mortem,* acquiring an absolute quality, is the profound sense of "damnation" (it is the "nothing" that burns in hell—Eckhart). When Schelling speaks, on this matter, of the soul descending "lower than nature," instead of elevating itself above nature and dominating it, he is hinting at an idea which, according to Heinrich, may find a correspondence in that of the "third place" of Hindu doctrine: that which is indicated in a symbolical form as a rebirth in forms of existence (in beings) that are lower than man.

In the case of positive essentification, both in Eckhart and in Schelling, one finds a metaphysical interpretation of the religious and eschatological myth of the "resurrection of the flesh." It is a "transfiguration" of the body itself, by means of which it unites itself with the soul, the corporeal making itself spiritual and the spiritual making itself corporeal in an indivisible unity. (Eckhart: "the essence of the body will be one with the essence of the soul in the divine essentiality.") This is the concept of the spiritual body, or glorious body, which we find also in St. Paul, who took it from the traditions of the ancient Mysteries. The Hindu parallel is the idea of *siddhakaya*, of the perfect body or magical body (*mayakaya*). Here we have again the parallelism between eschatology and initiatic doctrine, given that according to Hindu teaching this "resurrection of the body" is not necessarily to be placed at "the end of time," but can even be actuated during life by means of a special Yoga (one can find corresponding ideas in Chinese Taoism as well). In Eckhart and Schelling one does not meet any theory of this kind. In the first place, one can find only the correspondence with the *jivanmukti,* that is, with an absolute liberation that can be achieved in life (on the basis of the saying: "here and now it is the principle of eternal life" — *Jezunt ist des evigen lebens anevanc*). However, this is a perspective which already goes beyond the exoteric-religious view. In fact, Christianity as a whole has denied a similar possibility because it has moved eventual divinization to the *post mortem,* not to mention the "resurrection of the flesh," which it knows only in its mythical-eschatological form.

Along these lofty lines, the problem arises concerning the means by which one may conceive of a personal immortality, according to the need often manifested in the Western world, a need to which theism seems to cater. Heinrich justly notes how difficult it is to produce precise conceptual formulations when one is dealing with states and experiences where all the usual logical categories and discursive concepts cease to count (because of this, and with reason, Buddha refused categorically to speak in positive terms of *nirvana*). He states that in the same way that the supreme state, the *turiya,* is conceived of in the Vedanta as superior to both being and non-being, one must equally surpass here the antithesis between personal and impersonal. In this case, perhaps the best solution is given by the concept of "potentiality" or of "potency." At the terminal point of the way of liberation and transfiguration there is no longer the "person" but the potentiality, or potency, of being a genuine person: that is to say, no longer undergoing the restrictive condition of the "person," one may become a genuine person as the form in which a principle that, in itself, is superpersonal and free may occasionally manifest itself, without undergoing conditions of any kind. Schelling too speaks of this, in general terms, when he refers to an ultimate state in which "the infinite can become completely finite without damaging its infinity"; of which he likes to see a symbol in the Christological myth, in the incarnation of God, of the Father, in Christ. In more concrete terms, this idea is already contained in the concept of the "perfect body" or "body of resurrection," of which we have spoken.

There is lacking in Western examples a correspondence to the Hindu doctrine of the preexistence of the soul. Heinrich notes that in Schelling, the practical content of this doctrine is present in the idea of "transcendental character" anterior to manifestation in space and time, and as such might have the same role as the *samskara,* understood as that component of being which derives from an extra-biological heredity.

We will dwell no longer on the concordance of ideas in Vedanta, Eckhart, and Schelling, illustrated with clarity and acuteness by Heinrich, because this would lead to endless elaboration. The reader who is interested would do well to refer directly to the book. As we have said, one of its greatest virtues is the wealth of direct quotations from the texts (in those of Eckhart, a translation from Middle High to Modern German is given in the notes). To conclude, let us here make some considerations on the plane to which such comparisons refer.

This plane is essentially that of formal doctrinal correspondences, now more and now less complete. These correspondences must not hide the profound differences that exist from the existential point of view, because with Vedanta, with Eckhart, and with Schelling we find ourselves on three very different levels. The level of Vedanta is that of a metaphysical and esoteric (one might even say initiatory) tradition, in every way superpersonal. Eckhart's level is, on the other hand, that of mysticism, in metaphysical conclusions owed to the exceptional personality of the master, which do not occur in the frame of a tradition but, on the contrary, almost in opposition to the tradition which has served as a foundation (Christianity): whence the condemnation as "heresy" of some of Eckhart's most significant theses. It is true that in his writings mention is often made of "masters" ("a master says . . ."); but one must exclude (here and in general in the case of mystics) a transmission of doctrine, of techniques, and of spiritual influences, such as is the case in Hinduism. We are referred to ecstasies that Eckhart experienced, in a state of apparent death, as in certain forms of yogic *samadhi.* There is nothing similar in the case of Schelling, through whom we find ourselves on the plane of a philosophy of religion, that is, of speculation. The influence of Jacob Boehme may have played a certain part in Schelling, and he knew also the very first, imperfect translations of Oriental texts. But it appears clear that the antecedent here was essentially constituted by post-Kantian Idealistic philosophy, which, even though in him it does not reduce itself to a "philosophy for professors of professors of philosophy" (according to the malicious but pregnant description of Schopenhauer), remains nevertheless merely "philosophy." We find little more than simple conceptual formulations, in which the similarities with doctrines of traditional and esoteric character are only formal, owed to intuitions and not to an existential base. In some works that we wrote many years ago about "magical idealism," we ourselves showed that the whole current of critical Idealism (or, as it is also called, Absolute Idealism), having Kant as its starting point, finds itself facing the necessity of taking a "qualitative leap" if it truly wishes to resolve its most essential problems: it must transcend the plane of philosophical speculation and the limits of discursive thought, which is the same thing as saying the plane of modern profane thinking as a whole. One cannot deny that Schelling himself felt this when, in speaking of Boehme, he distinguished the "negative philosophy," which is that which is rational, speculative, and dialectical, from "positive philosophy," which is that which bases itself on experience, and, in part, on a superior experience. The second—he says—is "a kind of empiricism" in which "the supersensible becomes the object of a real experience" (rather than of abstract thought). Further, there is the aforementioned doctrine of "intellectual intuition." But all that, we repeat, reduces itself to a simple formulation, and in the West we have had no development of it in this direction on the plane of practical realization. Idealistic philosophy in particular has completely ignored these positions of Schelling, and has wound up in post-Hegelian historicism.

In another case, the phenomenology of Husserl has reaffirmed the need to make the center fall on direct experience: the "phenomenological reduction" should liberate experience from everything with which speculation, tradition, and current ideas have covered it in order to realize the phenomenon as a revelation of essence, starting from the center of light constituted by the "transcendental ego." In this school one sees again theoretical outlooks that form a parallel with Oriental and traditional "experimental metaphysics" and practice, but in phenomenology these are once more abstract, logical, psychological researches, researches for professional writers on philosophy and university teachers.

Heinrich concludes his excellent work with some rather optimistic phrases, with which we cannot entirely agree. He does not evaluate the correspondences ascertained from a merely doctrinal point of view, and thinks that they should not only concern the problem of Orient and Occident. They should also be the proof of the existence of a *catena aurea,* that is, of a continuity that does not concern only personal and philosophical speculations, but a sacred tradition that did not end in the late Middle Ages (Meister Eckhart), which is witnessed also in much more recent periods (Schelling), and which "even in the dark days with which the cruel history of humanity is filled" in the West, should be for us "the source of an indestructible certainty." We, however, believe that the continuity here spoken of has already ceased to exist in the West for a long time, and that, except for some rare subterranean veins not easy to define, in the Occident one may only speak of some isolated and almost accidental culmination, while today even the Orient seems to find itself far from the path of its most ancient and lofty traditions. In regard to the treasure of a transcendent wisdom, superior to that which is simply religion or philosophy, and the corresponding practical ways on the existential and practical plane, we believe that the idea of the *catena aurea* is of little help; we believe that for the situation of modern man, there may rather be applied the image used by us in one of our books: that of lost men who find themselves in a deserted and devastated region, and, aided only by an old, torn map, incomplete and hardly readable, must by their own efforts try to join the bulk of an army that has already moved on.

East & West, vol. 9, nos. 2 & 3 (1960): pp. 182–86

INDEX

ABOUT THE AUTHOR

JULIUS EVOLA, 1898–1974, was an Italian philosopher and esotericist who became one of the major exponents of the Traditionalist school of René Guénon. From the 1920s to 1945, Evola hoped that Italian Fascism, the Romanian Iron Guard, and German National Socialism could offer both a critique and rectification of the problems of the modern world consistent with Traditionalism. After the disaster of 1945, Evola withdrew from active political engagement, but his teachings continued to influence subsequent generations of thinkers and political actors on the Right, including the European and North American New Right movements.

His books include *Revolt Against the Modern World* (1934), *Heathen Imperialism* (1928), *The Hermetic Tradition: Symbols and Teachings of the Royal Art* (1931), *The Mystery of the Grail: Initiation and Magic in the Quest for the Spirit* (1937), *The Doctrine of Awakening: The Attainment of Self-Mastery According to the Earliest Buddhist Texts* (1943), *The Yoga of Power: Tantra, Shakti, and the Secret Way* (1949), *Men Among the Ruins: Post-War Reflections of a Radical Traditionalist* (1953), *The Metaphysics of Sex* (1958), and *Ride the Tiger: A Survival Manual for the Aristocrats of the Soul* (1961).

ABOUT THE EDITORS

GREG JOHNSON, Ph.D. is the author of *Confessions of a Reluctant Hater* (Counter-Currents, 2010; second ed., 2016), *New Right vs. Old Right* (Counter-Currents, 2013), *Truth, Justice, & a Nice White Country* (Counter-Currents, 2015), and *In Defense of Prejudice* (Counter-Currents, 2017).

COLLIN CLEARY, Ph.D. is the author of *Summoning the Gods: Essays on Paganism in a God-Forsaken World* (Counter-Currents, 2011) and *What is a Rune? And Other Essays* (Counter-Currents, 2015).